KANTIAN TRANSPOSITIONS

KANTIAN TRANSPOSITIONS

Derrida and the Philosophy of Religion

Eddis N. Miller

Northwestern University Press
Evanston, Illinois

Northwestern University Press
www.nupress.northwestern.edu

First paperback printing 2019.

Printed in the United States of America

10 9 8 7 6 5 4 3 2 1

ISBN 978-0-8101-4092-9 (paper)

The Library of Congress has cataloged the original, hardcover edition as follows:

Miller, Eddis N., author.
Kantian transpositions : Derrida and the philosophy of religion / Eddis N. Miller.
pages cm
Includes bibliographical references and index.
ISBN 978-0-8101-2980-1 (cloth : alk. paper)
Includes bibliographical references and index.
1. Religion—Philosophy. 2. Derrida, Jacques—Religion. 3. Faith and reason. 4. Kant, Immanuel, 1724–1804—Influence. 5. Kant, Immanuel, 1724–1804—Religion. I. Title.

BL51.M6265 2014
210—dc23

2014007640

For Lisa

Contents

Acknowledgments

I would like to thank the two anonymous readers for their helpful comments on the manuscript, as well as the editorial staff at Northwestern University Press for all of their hard work.

I owe a special debt of gratitude to Jean-Michel Rabaté. It was in his seminar on "The Gift in Theory and Literature" that I first began to think seriously about Derrida's writings on religion, and he was my primary adviser when this project was a dissertation at the University of Pennsylvania. Had Jean-Michel not graciously agreed to supervise my work, this book, and perhaps my PhD, would not exist.

I have had the fortune to be sustained and distracted by a number of great friends, including Gerry Romeo, Matt Belcher, and J Melvin. Adam Graves has been a constant intellectual companion; this book profited enormously from his loud, animated, and incisive responses to my ideas. Perhaps no one would have been happier to see this work finally come to fruition than Stephen Gardner, whose humor, brilliance, and sensitivity will remain for me unrivalled.

Everything I have accomplished has been made possible by the unwavering love and support of my family. I thank my parents, particularly for never looking at me quizzically at any stage of this rather odd journey, and my grandmother, for inspiring in me a deep love of the written word.

My wife, Lisa Anderson, has been at the center of everything good in my life for the past ten years. This book belongs to her as much as it does to me, if not more. I asked her to read this manuscript a truly cruel number of times, and she did so willingly and expertly; any style or grace to be found in this book is due entirely to her.

Introduction

> Le tout est de savoir de quel "Kant" on parle.
> —Jean-Luc Nancy

Analytic philosophy of religion has moved along more or less unimpeded by the Kantian critique of speculative theology—and, it could be added, in a state of obliviousness to the Heideggerian destruction of onto-theology. But what goes under the name of "continental philosophy of religion" has proceeded along very different lines. In a sense, continental philosophy of religion in the twentieth century has been a repetition of philosophy of religion in the eighteenth. Just as Kant's attack on traditional speculative theology was followed by his own attempt to re-ground God and religion by way of practical reason, so too has Heidegger's destruction of onto-theology—a term coined by Kant himself—been followed by any number of attempts to think about God outside of the confines of metaphysics; and, unsurprisingly, one of the ways in which twentieth-century continental philosophy has sought to re-access God and religion is by way of ethics.

The works of Jacques Derrida have been at the center of such attempts, and Kant's philosophy of religion occupies an important place, as I will show, in Derrida's texts on religion. Of these texts, one of the most important and programmatic is "Faith and Knowledge: The Two Sources of 'Religion' at the Limits of Reason Alone," published in 1996. The importance of the Kantian reference in this text runs much deeper than the playfulness of the title, which implicates not only Kant's *Religion within the Limits of Reason Alone,* but also Hegel's *Faith and Knowledge* and Bergson's *The Two Sources of Morality and Religion.* In "Faith and Knowledge," originally presented at a seminar in Capri in 1994, Derrida asks, "*what of this 'Kantian' gesture today? What would a book be like today which, like Kant's, is entitled,* Religion within the Limits of Reason Alone?" Derrida says that the task of those gathered in Capri consists in nothing less than the "*attempt to transpose, here and now, the circumspect and suspensive attitude, a certain* epoché *that consists—rightly or wrongly, for the issue is serious—in thinking religion or making it appear 'within the limits of reason alone.'*"[1]

But what, precisely, does it mean to "transpose" the "Kantian" gesture of thinking religion "within the limits of reason alone"? Is this transposition a simple repetition of the Kantian gesture? And in what does Derrida understand this Kantian gesture to consist? The thesis of this book is that an understanding of "Faith and Knowledge," and, therefore, an understanding of Derrida's engagement with religion more broadly, requires us not only to understand what Derrida means by "transposing" the "Kantian" gesture, but also to read "Faith and Knowledge" precisely as an attempt to enact such a transposition. More specifically, I will demonstrate that this "transposition" does not involve the mere shift of a word, concept, or philosopheme from one context to another, a simple repetition of the Kantian gesture. Rather, what Derrida transposes is not the gesture of "Kant as such," as if there were one, self-identical gesture to which this proper name could be attached, but rather the gesture of a "certain Kant."

What does it mean to speak of a "certain Kant"? The phrase "a certain X" appears frequently in Derrida's writings, and is in fact a consequence of the fundamental deconstructive insight that the texts of the philosophical tradition are unable to maintain the rigorous purity of their conceptual delimitations and determinations. A deconstructive reading of the texts of the philosophical tradition therefore follows the suppression, marginalization, and disavowal of those elements that contaminate this supposed purity. If the Kantian critique involves drawing the boundaries of reason, then an attempt to rethink the Kantian heritage must begin, in Derrida's words, by "bringing to light those effects of authority that are already, strictly, 'within' (if one can put it this way, for the language is still Kantian) his oeuvre, by studying its hierarchizing, canonizing, marginalizing, and disqualifying procedures, the 'internal' structuring of the text, the exclusion (that is, the externalizing) of the Opuscules, Parerga, or Remarks."[2] This play of "within" and "without" is crucial; if the Kantian critique can only maintain its mastery over its own conceptual delimitations through the marginalization of those elements that threaten the rigor of these delimitations, then the deconstructive lever for the Kantian text is already provided, as it were, by the Kantian text itself. Derrida writes: "The Kantian heritage is not only the Kantian heritage, a thing identical to itself. Like every heritage, it exceeds itself to provide (or lay claim to) the analysis of this heritage and, better, the instruments of analysis for every heritage. This 'supplementary' structure must be taken into account. A heritage always surreptitiously bequeaths to us the means of interpreting it."[3]

This is why Derrida speaks of a "certain Kant." The lever for a deconstructive reading is found within the text itself (which is why deconstruction is not something that someone does to a text or imposes from without). There is no one "Kant," but a multiplicity of voices within Kant's text. Naturally, this undermines the reliability of "Kant" as a proper name. It will always be a matter, as Nancy says, of knowing of which "Kant" one is speaking.

To return, then, to the question of "transposition," if Derrida transposes the Kantian gesture of thinking religion "within the limits of reason alone," the "Kant" who will be transposed here is a deconstructive and deconstructed Kant, one who finally cannot master the limits and boundaries that he erects. "Faith and Knowledge," therefore, will be a text that, in its turn, will transpose the gesture of thinking religion within the limits of reason alone, but without simply repeating it. It will repeat it, in other words, with a *difference,* a difference that can only be fully appreciated through a careful examination of Derrida's various engagements, in "Faith and Knowledge" and beyond it, with Kant's philosophy of religion.

As will become clear in Chapter 2 and Chapter 4 of this book, Derrida's transposition of Kant's notion of "reflective faith" is central to his strategy in "Faith and Knowledge." But the centrality of this notion of reflective faith—and indeed the necessity of reading "Faith and Knowledge" as a whole as a "Kantian transposition"—remains, to the best of my knowledge, unexplored in Derrida scholarship. This is clearly the case, for example, in two of the most important books on Derrida's writings on religion, John Caputo's *The Prayers and Tears of Jacques Derrida,* and Hent de Vries' *Philosophy and the Turn to Religion.* While they are and will no doubt remain indispensable studies of Derrida and religion, they do not address the significance of Derrida's claim to be transposing the "Kantian" gesture of thinking religion within the limits of reason alone.

The same holds true, more recently, for Michael Naas's thoroughgoing analysis of Derrida's "Faith and Knowledge" (an analysis "*à la Guéroult*")[4] in *Miracle and Machine: Jacques Derrida and the Two Sources of Religion, Science, and the Media.* Taking note of the sustained attention Derrida pays to Kant in this text, Naas writes: "The fact that Derrida ends up devoting much more of his time to Kant's *Religion* than to Hegel's *Faith and Knowledge* may tell us something about where Derrida's sympathies or at least his interests lie [. . .]."[5] This book will demonstrate that Kant's place in "Faith and Knowledge" constitutes something much more significant than sympathy or interest, and, indeed, that the "Kantian" dimension of the text is absolutely central to Derrida's project.

It is safe to say that as Derrida's star has fallen within the literature programs in which deconstruction originally found its home in the United States, his star has risen among theologians and philosophers of religion (of the continental variety) who are not only drawn to Derrida's texts on religion and ethics—texts that certainly became more abundant toward the end of his life—but also find in deconstruction generally new resources for thinking about God and religion in the wake of the supposed demise of metaphysics.[6] While some have contested such religious or theological appropriation, there is of course nothing to prevent Derrida's texts from being put to this use; indeed, the inevitable susceptibility of these texts to all kinds of appropriation and expropriation is one of the basic lessons of deconstruction.

It is not my concern, in the present text, to contest the validity or usefulness of such readings. Instead, I will take a rather different angle, reading Derrida's late texts on religion as an *interrogation of the meaning and possibility of philosophy of religion as a philosophical discipline.* Any such interrogation must proceed—as it in fact does proceed, in Derrida's writings—by way of an engagement with Kant, and this because of Kant's pivotal role in the foundation of philosophy of religion as a philosophical discipline.

The plan of this book is as follows. In Chapter 1, I historically situate Kant at the origin of the discipline of "philosophy of religion"; then, by way of preparation for an examination of Derrida's reading of Kant, I address the meaning and importance of Kant's ethicotheology, as well as his philosophical hermeneutic in the *Religion.* Specifically, I demonstrate that the God of Kant's ethicotheology is a *spectral God.* In Chapter 2, I proceed to Derrida's reading of Kant's philosophy of religion, not only in "Faith and Knowledge," but also in a number of earlier texts, including "Parergon" (from *Truth in Painting*), *Glas,* and some unpublished seminar material from the time of *Glas.* It is vital to understand Derrida's deconstruction of the Kantian gesture of thinking religion within the limits of reason alone in these texts in order to fully appreciate Derrida's transposition of this gesture in "Faith and Knowledge."

Chapter 3 takes a necessary detour into Derrida's reading of Kant's ethics. Derrida's various engagements with Kant's ethics are not only interesting in their own right; they are vital to my argument. Derrida's texts on religion cannot be understood independently of his thinking about ethics, for which Kant's ethics play a pivotal role. While Levinas has certainly been the name most readily associated with Derrida's writings on ethics (and not without warrant), I nevertheless demonstrate in Chapter 3 that the aporia of ethics for Derrida derives from a mutually necessary and yet mutually incompatible "Kantianism" and "Levinasianism."

Despite appearances, Kant plays as vital a role as Levinas in Derrida's thinking about ethics. Moreover, I argue here that while we cannot speak of "Derrida's ethics" or an "ethics of deconstruction," since "ethics" for Derrida is strictly speaking impossible, this *does not* mean, *contra* Martin Hägglund, that there is no prescriptive moment in Derrida's texts.

Finally, in Chapter 4, I examine Derrida's transposition itself in "Faith and Knowledge." Specifically, I demonstrate how the Kantian notion of "reflective faith," which serves as a lever for Derrida's deconstructive reading of Kant's *Religion*, becomes the banner, as it were, under which Derrida's transposition of Kant is carried out. This point will be crucial for understanding a number of themes in "Faith and Knowledge"—faith, holiness, sacrifice, radical evil, and hospitality—and particularly for understanding the difficult yet central question of the relationship between revelation (*Offenbarung*) and revealability (*Offenbarkeit*), and its implications for the idea of messianicity.

KANTIAN TRANSPOSITIONS

1

A Minimum of Theology: Kant's Spectral God

I

The philosophy of religion, as Walter Jaeschke argues in *Reason in Religion: The Foundations of Hegel's Philosophy of Religion,* has a more difficult task than other disciplines that include the word "religion"—such as the history of religion or the sociology of religion—precisely because they are able to abstract from the question concerning the existence of God. Philosophy, on the other hand, is obliged to inquire into the very principles of its objects of inquiry. In a similar way, the difficulties faced by a philosophy of religion are different from those faced by a philosophy of art or of history, neither of which "is burdened with the difficulty that weighs on the philosophy of religion, namely that religion intends an actuality that lies beyond it and is thoroughly questionable, but through which alone it receives its sense and its right to exist."[1]

In Kant's time, the task of investigating the existence of God fell to metaphysics, which was traditionally divided into general metaphysics (or ontology), and special metaphysics, which comprised three disciplines, *theologia rationalis, psychologica rationalis,* and *cosmologica rationalis. Theologia naturalis* (rational theology) concerned itself with the question of God's existence. The "philosophy of religion" was then dependent upon the labor of rational theology. As Jaeschke writes:

> To engage in philosophy of religion appeared meaningful only because philosophical theology had removed all doubt concerning the question of God. And it was not only the different tasks assigned to philosophy of religion and philosophical theology but also their differing status that helped to determine the way in which they were regarded by such eighteenth-century school philosophers as Christian Wolff. The philosophical knowledge of God was seen as forming the culminating discipline of theoretical philosophy, whereas what could at all events be called philosophy of religion belonged to *philosophia practica.* At that time it embraced little more than was involved in defining one's *officia erga Deum.* Inasmuch as it was essentially confined to this, it also did not

> count as an independent philosophical discipline but as part of ethics. The idea that, over and above this practical aspect, religion is capable of philosophical treatment in the framework of an independent subdiscipline was, toward the end of the eighteenth century, still open to contention—the more plausibly so because up to then the very term "philosophy of religion" had been quite unknown.[2]

It was late in the eighteenth century, then, that a new conception of the philosophy of religion emerged and broke free of its previously marginal position within philosophy, and first received its name: *philosophia* or *theoria religionis.*[3]

Why, precisely, did this new conception of the "philosophy of religion" emerge? The reason can be located in Kant's philosophical revolution.[4] What is at stake here is not a "transformation" of natural theology into the philosophy of religion. "The relation between philosophical theology and philosophy of religion at the beginning of the nineteenth century is rather to be understood as conditioned by the demonstration of the impossibility of the one discipline and its replacement by another, whose contents and methods differ widely from those espoused previously."[5] Kant, having demonstrated the failure of traditional philosophical theology in the first *Critique,*[6] attempted to re-ground the idea of God through practical philosophy. This new foundation "was not open to the critique directed at the proofs of God, the foundation of traditional natural theology, but it was wholly suited to provide the fledgling philosophy of religion with the foundations it needed if it was not to forgo the idea of God, and with it the very crux of the concept of religion."[7]

Kant attempted to provide a philosophical basis for the idea of God by way of the notion of a "postulate of practical reason." Kant's doctrine of the postulates, which include not only the idea of God, but the ideas of freedom and immortality as well, underwent a number of changes throughout the course of his career, making it difficult to offer a simple account of the meaning and function of the postulates. Nevertheless, before proceeding to an examination of the specific task of Kant's *Religion within the Limits of Reason Alone,* I will examine more closely the concept of a "postulate of practical reason," since it is on this concept that Kant's entire ethicotheology—and, therefore, the new discipline of "philosophy of religion"—is based.

II

In the *Lectures on the Philosophical Doctrine of Religion*, Kant asks what would be the *minimum requirement* for a theology, and he concludes that this minimum of theology is the idea that God is *possible*.[8] What Kant has not yet realized, at this stage of his ethicotheology, is that this possible God constitutes not only the minimum of theology, but its maximum as well; in other words, God can only ever be—from the perspective of human knowledge—possible.[9] This is not simply for the reason, derived from the most basic principles of Kant's transcendental idealism, that God's existence is not an object of possible human cognition and therefore remains at most, and at least, a possibility. Rather, while the existence of God must be possible, or else it could not be postulated by practical reason, God must remain only a possibility if the idea of God is to be conducive to morality rather than a threat to it. The limits of theoretical knowledge, then, represent a blessing of sorts, indeed an advantage, from the perspective of humanity's moral vocation; and nature, which at first blush appears to have bestowed cognitive faculties upon us in a most "stepmotherly fashion,"[10] shows, upon further reflection, to have wisely adapted our cognitive faculties to our moral vocation. Were we to have absolutely certain knowledge of God's existence, as Kant suggests in the second *Critique*, our very ability to act morally would be compromised:

> Instead of the conflict that the moral disposition now has to carry on with the inclinations, in which, though after some defeats, moral strength of soul is to be gradually acquired, *God and eternity with their awful majesty* would stand unceasingly *before our eyes* (for what we can prove perfectly holds as much certainty for us as what we are assured of by our sight). Transgression of the law would, no doubt, be avoided: what is commanded would be done; but because the *disposition* from which actions ought to be done cannot be instilled by any command, and because the spur to activity in this case would be promptly at hand and *external*, reason would have no need to work itself up so as to gather strength to resist the inclinations by a lively representation of the dignity of the law: hence most actions conforming to the law would be done from fear, only a few from hope, and none at all from duty, and the moral worth of actions, on which alone in the eyes of supreme wisdom the worth of the person and even that of the world depends, would not exist at all. As long as human nature remains as it is, human conduct would thus be changed into mere mechanism in which, as in a puppet show, everything would *gesticulate* well but there would be *no life* in the figures.[11]

Were we assured of God's existence—were we to have true theoretical knowledge that God is not merely possible, but actual—the "awful majesty" of this living God could not but inspire terror; and since it is above all essential that our actions not be determined pathologically, but solely by respect for the moral law, theoretical knowledge of God would threaten to undermine moral action.

Kant could very well have concluded, on the basis of this line of thought, that moral action and belief in God are simply incompatible—provided, that is, that God is understood to be a dispenser of reward and punishment on the basis of his pleasure or displeasure with human actions (an understanding of God that is indeed central to much of his ethicotheology). Kant never draws any such conclusion; yet it nevertheless remains that the moral principle, as Kant determines it, must be able to function in the radical absence of God—an absence that is implied in the very idea of God as a postulate of practical reason.[12] God is not, and cannot be, the source of the moral law; Kant rejects all such heteronomy in the name of a self-legislating (autonomous) reason. It is only *after* this death of God—this suspension of his existence in the formation of the moral principle—that a concept of God can be constructed that functions wholly in accord with the moral principle, and in such a way that the *ends* of moral action find their fulfillment. Yet, if the living God must undergo a death in the name of the moral principle, then the God that is resurrected out of practical reason is no longer the original, living God, but one who dwells between life and death, existence and non-existence; in short, the God of ethicotheology is a *spectral God.*

In its most schematic form, Kant's argument for the postulates of practical reason proceeds as follows. The moral law commands that human beings set as their goal or ultimate end the attainment of the highest good. Moreover, in order for a human to rationally pursue such an end, it must be possible for this end to be attained. But the possibility of the attainment of the highest good requires the postulation of the existence of God, freedom, and immortality. Therefore, even though God, freedom, and immortality are not possible objects of human knowledge (and therefore capable of no apodictic proof, as Kant demonstrates in the first *Critique*), nevertheless reason in its practical capacity can postulate the existence of these objects, as they are necessary for the realization of the end commanded by the moral law.

The first component of this argument that calls for commentary is the concept of the highest good itself. While the moral law commands us unconditionally to act virtuously, which is to say, to act out of respect for the moral law, regardless of what other ends may be attained through such action, it is nevertheless the case, as Kant maintains, that virtuous action is not the *complete* good for a finite rational being. Kant writes:

> That *virtue* (as worthiness to be happy) is the *supreme condition* of whatever can even seem to us desirable and hence of all our pursuit of

> happiness and that it is therefore the *supreme* good has been proven in the Analytic. But it is not yet, on that account, the whole and complete good as the object of the faculty of desire of rational finite beings; for this, *happiness* is also required, and that not merely in the partial eyes of a person who makes himself an end but even in the judgment of an impartial reason, which regards a person in the world generally as an end in itself.[13]

Human beings as *rational* beings are motivated to virtue by the moral law itself, which commands unconditionally; but as *finite* beings, i.e., beings endowed with sensibility, they also seek the satisfaction of their inclinations. Kant defines happiness precisely as the "satisfaction of all our inclinations."[14] Therefore as beings both finite and rational, humans are oriented both toward the fulfillment of the moral law and the pursuit of happiness.

The highest good, then, consists in the union of virtue and happiness, and insofar as humans are both rational and finite beings, the object of their willing must consist in the attainment of the highest good. But how are these two to be combined? This is precisely the question Kant asks in the second *Critique*, in the "Antinomy of Practical Reason." The combination of these two concepts (virtue and happiness), Kant says, must be either analytic (a logical connection between the two concepts) or synthetic (a real, causal connection between the two concepts). As Kant puts it:

> The connection of virtue with happiness can therefore be understood in one of two ways: either the endeavor to be virtuous and the rational pursuit of happiness are not two different actions but quite identical, in which case no maxim need be made the ground of the former other than that which serves for the latter; or else that connection is found in virtue's producing happiness as something different from the consciousness of virtue, as a cause produces an effect.[15]

Kant rejects an analytic connection between the two, since virtue and happiness are logically distinct and indeed heterogeneous concepts.[16] So their relationship must be synthetic, which is to say, "either the desire for happiness must be the motive to maxims of virtue or the maxim of virtue must be the efficient cause of happiness." The antinomy of practical reason arises because, as Kant shows, both formulations are unacceptable. The first thesis is "*absolutely* impossible because [. . .] maxims that put the determining ground of the will in the desire for one's happiness are not moral at all and can be the ground of no virtue."[17] In other words, the moral worth of an action consists solely in acting out of respect for the law; therefore, acting on the maxim of happiness immediately precludes the action from having any moral worth. On the other hand, the idea that virtue is the efficient cause of happiness is equally misguided, since

> any practical connection of causes and effects in the world, as a result of the determination of the will, does not depend on the moral disposition of the will but upon knowledge of the laws of nature and the physical ability to use them for one's purposes; consequently, no necessary connection of happiness with virtue in the world, adequate to the highest good, can be expected from the most meticulous observation of laws.[18]

In other words, in the realm of nature (the domain of cause and effect), happiness does not result from moral action but rather from the knowledge of the laws of nature and the ability to exploit these laws to one's own advantage. Pragmatic knowledge results in the satisfaction of inclinations, not moral behavior. It seems, therefore, that there can be no hope of possibly attaining the highest good, even though the moral law commands us to set it as our end. Happiness in accordance with virtue (or, as Kant glosses it, the worthiness to be happy) seems a mere fantasy.

As a solution to this antinomy, Kant formulates the notion of the postulates of practical reason. The postulates are threefold: the immortality of the soul, the existence of God, and freedom. But in fact, as Paul Guyer has argued, the respective functions of these three postulates are in fact quite different; they do not all serve to connect virtue and happiness. Indeed, freedom is not really a postulate of practical reason at all, but is rather the condition of any moral action whatsoever, since an action can only be said to be moral or immoral in the first place, according to Kant, if it is a free act imputable to a human being. If one's actions are the result of some coercive force or other that one does not have the freedom to resist, then it makes no sense to say that such actions are moral or immoral. The postulation of freedom, then, does not pertain specifically to the attainment of the highest good, but is rather the *conditio sine qua non* of any moral action whatsoever.[19]

Kant's argument for immortality runs as follows. The highest good is the necessary object of a will as commanded by the moral law. But the attainment of the highest good presupposes the "*complete* conformity of the dispositions with the moral law." Such conformity must be possible, therefore, for the highest good to be possible. But since a complete conformity amounts to "*holiness,* a perfection of which no rational being of the sensible world is capable at any moment of his existence," this conformity can only be the end result of an "endless progress" toward it.

This endless progress, however, presupposes that "the *existence* and personality of the same rational being continu[e] *endlessly* (which is called the immortality of the soul)."[20]

This postulate is only required if one assumes, as Kant does here, that moral perfection consists not simply in acting out of respect for the moral law in all cases—despite any inclinations one might experience to the contrary—but in a state of holiness wherein one not only acts out of respect for the moral law, but never experiences any inclinations that run counter to it.[21] But there is a fundamental problem with this idea of holiness. Holiness is required in order to make possible the highest good. But the highest good is the object not of a purely rational will—which does not partake of sensibility and therefore has as its sole object of volition the moral law itself—but of a finite will which acts not simply with a view to virtue but also to happiness as the satisfaction of inclinations. Therefore, making holiness a condition of the highest good would be absurd, because a purely rational holy will does not aim at the satisfaction of inclinations, which belong only to a finite, sensible being.[22] Simply stated, happiness is irrelevant for a holy will, since such a will does not have inclinations to satisfy and therefore take as the object of its will not happiness, but the moral law alone. The notion of the highest good does not, then, *contra* Kant, presuppose a holy will (and therefore the postulate of immortality), but in fact disallows it. Thus the problem with the postulate of immortality is not simply that it holds too stringent a notion of moral perfection; the very idea that the highest good requires the postulate of immortality is incoherent.[23] Moreover, as Jaeschke argues, even if the notion of the highest good did demand holiness, immortality would not make holiness possible anyway, since even an *infinite* approximation of an unattainable ideal does not bring the will any closer to attaining it.[24]

This leaves the postulate of God's existence, the only postulate of practical reason required by, and specifically responding to, the antinomy of practical reason. The need to postulate God's existence as a condition of possibility of the realization of the highest good is presented by Kant as follows. The moral law should be, for a rational being, the determining ground of the will, independent of any other incentives. Assuming that this is the case, happiness would be the state in which nature harmonizes with the ends of this being's will (happiness) as well as the determining grounds of its will (the moral law). But there is no reason to think that morality as the determining ground of the will produces any effects in the natural world, since the freedom through which the moral law commands is independent of the causality of nature. Consequently, there is no necessary connection between virtue as the worthiness to be happy and actual happiness in this world. And yet, such a connection between happiness and virtue must be possible. The only way to make such a connection possible is to postulate "the existence of a cause of nature, distinct from nature, which contains the ground of this connection, namely of the exact correspondence of happiness with morality."[25] The existence of God, therefore, as the author of nature, is postulated to ensure the attainment of happiness in accordance with one's worthiness of it, a worthiness attained only through acting out of respect for the moral law alone. Kant concludes:

> Now, a being capable of actions in accordance with the representation of laws is *an intelligence* (a rational being), and the causality of such a being in accordance with this representation of laws is his *will.* Therefore the supreme cause of nature, insofar as it must be presupposed for the highest good, is a being that is the cause of nature by *understanding* and *will* (hence its author), that is, **God.**[26]

Not only is God, as postulated by practical reason, the intelligent cause of nature; Kant also attributes to this God all of the features attributed to him by classical speculative theology. In the first *Critique,* Kant specifies that this divine will

> must be omnipotent, so that all of nature and its relation to morality in the world are subject to it; omniscient, so that it cognizes the inmost dispositions and their moral worth; omnipresent, so that it is immediately ready for every need that is demanded by the highest good for the world; eternal, so that this agreement of nature and freedom is not lacking at any time, etc.[27]

Thus the attributes of God as a postulate of practical reason effectively mirror the attributes of the God of philosophical theology. Moreover, the antinomy of practical reason is effectively resolved, since the existence of God makes possible a causality different from the causality of nature. There is a synthetic connection between virtue and happiness because God can grant happiness in accordance with one's worthiness of it, which is to say, God can create the conditions wherein virtue *causes* happiness. Thus, since God is necessary for the highest good, the pursuit of which is commanded by the moral law itself, Kant can conclude that it is "morally necessary to assume the existence of God."[28]

What remains to be considered, however, is the precise status of this moral proof of God's existence. What exactly is Kant's achievement here vis-à-vis speculative theology? Does the practical postulation of God's existence amount to a *proof* of God's existence? To begin to formulate an answer to this question, let us return to the original antinomy of practical reason that generated the need for the postulates in the first place. After showing that the analytic and synthetic understandings of the connection between virtue and happiness both fail, Kant underscores what is at stake in this antinomy:

> Now, since the promotion of the highest good, which contains this connection in its concept, is an a priori necessary object of our will and inseparably bound up with the moral law, the impossibility of the first must also prove the falsity of the second. If, therefore, the highest good is impossible in accordance with practical rules, then the moral law, which commands us to promote it, must be fantastic and directed to empty imaginary ends and must therefore in itself be false.[29]

It is indeed possible to understand this passage as making the claim that the validity of the moral law depends on the *possibility* of the realization of the highest good. And since the possibility of the highest good requires the postulation of God, then it follows that God is necessary to ground the validity of the moral law. According to this interpretation, Kant's argument would be hopelessly circular: God is postulated on the basis of a moral law that is only valid on the assumption that God exists.[30] The problem with this interpretation is that it fails to take into account Kant's extensive argumentation, throughout the *Groundwork* and the "Analytic of Practical Reason" in the second *Critique*, for his claim that the moral law objectively determines the will of every rational being regardless of the end to be obtained. The moral law, in other words, grounds itself, and does not require God for its validity. An interpretation of this passage, therefore, that sees the postulate of God as necessary to ground the validity of the moral law ignores the main thrust of Kant's ethical arguments.[31] Nevertheless, the question remains how one is to understand Kant's comment in the second *Critique* that without the possibility of realizing the highest good (which ultimately demands the postulation of God's existence), the moral law "must be fantastic and directed to empty imaginary ends and must therefore be in itself false."

A correct interpretation of Kant's argument concerning the postulates of practical reason must take into consideration the fact that, while the moral law is unconditionally binding for a rational being, it is nevertheless the case that the human being is not purely rational; according to Kant's anthropology, humans are a mixture of rational and sensible natures. Insofar as it is rational, the human will is determined by the moral law. Insofar as it is finite and sensible, the human will is determined by the desire for happiness as the satisfaction of its inclinations. Inclinations are not universal among humans, and often conflict with one another; therefore, happiness cannot be the principle upon which a universal and binding ethics is based. To be truly universal and valid a priori, principles of action must be derived from the moral law alone. But as Kant argues, just because the moral law is the determining ground of the human will insofar as the human being is rational, it is nevertheless the case that, given finitude and sensibility, the moral law will never be the *sole* object of the human will. Happiness is an ineluctable object of the finite will. Kant is thus faced with the difficulty of reconciling the moral law with happiness. And it is the need for such reconciliation that, as we have seen, leads Kant to argue for God as the condition of possibility of such a reconciliation of morality and happiness. The key point, however, is that this problem of the realization of the highest good is set in motion by human finitude and sensibility, which necessarily has the satisfaction of its inclinations as the object of its will. For a purely rational being, no such reconciliation of morality and happiness would be required, because a purely rational being would not have the sensibility which demands the satisfaction of such inclinations. Therefore, the antinomy of practical reason that makes necessary the postulation of God's existence would never arise for a purely rational being. For such a being, the moral law completely determines the will, with no inclination to do otherwise. This is why Kant insists that a purely rational being does not experience the moral law in the form of an imperative, which is only the way that *finite* rational beings experience the moral law.[32] Now, since the antinomy of practical reason would not arise for a purely rational being, and thus neither would the postulates be necessary for such a being, one can see why the moral law in itself does not depend on the existence of God for its validity. Rather, God is a necessary postulate only because of the finitude of the human being, because the moral law is not the sole object of the will for the human being. In short, the postulation of God's existence is only necessary because of man's specific constitution as a sensible and finite creature. While this interpretation effectively saves Kant's ethics from being undermined in the absence of God's existence (in other words, the atheist is not freed from the obligation that the moral law entails), it does reduce the idea of God to a mere *anthropological idea.*

This anthropological function of Kant's postulates becomes more explicit, or perhaps less thinly veiled, in the third *Critique*. Here Kant makes it clear that the validity of the moral law is in no way threatened by the denial of God's existence: "This proof [. . .] is not meant to say that it is just as necessary to assume the existence of God as it is to acknowledge the validity of the moral law, hence that whoever cannot convince himself of the former can judge himself to be free from the obligations of the latter."[33] And in Section 90, "On the kind of affirmation involved in a moral proof of the existence of God," Kant asserts that the moral proof is indeed meant to convince, but then specifies that a proof that aims at conviction can be one of two kinds: "either one that would determine what the object is **in itself** or else one that would determine what it is **for us** (human beings in general) according to the necessary rational principles for our judging (a proof *kat' 'alētheian* or *kat' 'anthrōpon,* taking the latter word in the broadest sense to stand for human beings in general)."[34] This confirms the thesis that the postulates are necessitated by the constitution of the human being in its combination of rational and sensible natures, and not by reason as such.[35] It would be legitimate to claim, then, that the anthropological critique of religion in Feuerbach and Nietzsche, for example, is to a certain extent prepared by Kant's ethicotheology.[36]

There are, however, points at which Kant seems to overemphasize the achievement of his moral grounding of the idea of God; a good example of this can be found in the *Lectures on Philosophical Theology,* where Kant says, with a healthy degree of confidence in the moral proof:

> Moral theism is of course critical, since it pursues all the speculative proofs for the existence of God step by step, and recognizes them to be insufficient; indeed, the moral theist asserts absolutely that it is impossible for speculative reason to demonstrate the existence of such a being with apodictic certainty; but he is nevertheless firmly convinced of the existence of this being, and he has a faith beyond all doubt on practical grounds. The foundation on which he builds his faith is unshakeable and it can never be overthrown, not even if all human beings united to undermine it. It is a fortress in which the moral human being can find refuge with no fear of ever being driven from it, because every attack on it will come to nothing. Hence his faith in God built on this foundation is as certain as a mathematical demonstration.[37]

However one understands the status and efficacy of the moral proof, one must also distinguish between Kant's own impression of its success and the reception of this proof, which was to a large extent determined by Reinhold's *Letters on the Kantian Philosophy.* Reinhold had the merit of being aware of the more affirmative side to Kant's destruction of philosophical theology, but he overestimated the degree of certainty attained by means of this proof. For example, in the third letter, "The result of the Critique of Reason concerning the necessary connection between morality and religion," originally published in 1787 in *Der Teutsche Merkur,* Reinhold writes: "By the clearing away of these proofs in the manner accomplished by the Critique of Reason, religion gains nothing less than a single, unshakeable, and universally valid ground of cognition, one which completes by means of reason the unification of religion and morality that was introduced through Christianity by means of the heart." Later in the same letter, he writes: "The ground of cognition that [the ideas of pure practical reason] contain for the existence and the properties of the deity is thus not only as secure and unchanging as the essence of reason itself, but also as intuitive and illuminating as the self-consciousness that a human being has of his rational nature."[38] Thus the fact that Kant may not indeed have grounded a philosophy of religion with the apodictic certainty of the proofs of philosophical theology did not necessarily prevent his moral proof from being understood as having performed this function.

That Kant's postulates would be seen in the 1790s, which Jaeschke calls the "decade of the moral God,"[39] as an effective replacement of philosophical theology was perhaps inevitable, given Kant's language of a "moral proof." Kant invoked this language of proof quite often; and yet, he never ceased to underscore that this ethicotheology was fundamentally about "faith," albeit a rational one. This faith is rational insofar as it responds to a need of practical reason, and insofar as the object of this faith is determined strictly by way of these practical needs; nothing is predicated of God other than what practical reason requires. God's existence nevertheless remains an object of "faith" precisely because God cannot be an object of possible theoretical knowledge. Thus the idea of God given to the human being through this practical faith cannot be extended beyond the practical domain and employed speculatively.

But "moral proof" and "rational faith" are nevertheless two very different things, which Kant had a tendency to conflate, producing perplexing and nearly unreadable formulations like his claim in the third *Critique* that the moral argument "proves the existence of God only as a matter of faith for practical pure reason."[40] How exactly does one prove the existence of God as a matter of faith? Would not a proof obviate the need for faith? And would an object of faith need proof? This perplexing formulation is really a symptom of Kant's desire to stand on two sides of the fence. The postulation of God's existence is necessary to motivate the human as an imperfectly rational creature to subordinate his inclinations to the moral law and fulfill his moral vocation. And yet, Kant did not want to transgress the limits of knowledge he established in the first *Critique,* which rendered impossible any apodictic demonstration of God's existence. Thus, what Kant wanted to prove, ultimately, was that there is a good moral reason for believing in God. Such an argument would no doubt have little or no effect on someone previously indisposed to hold such a belief. Nevertheless, the argument could possibly have a positive moral effect on someone already disposed to such a belief. It is to such people that the postulates are ultimately directed.

This, then, is Kant's double bind. While the binding nature of the moral law cannot be contingent upon a promise of happiness, it remains the case that, in the face of human finitude, action cannot be entirely divorced from satisfaction of the inclinations. It is only God who is able to forge a connection between virtue and happiness. Belief in God, therefore, strengthens and supports the moral vocation of humanity. And yet, were this belief so strong as to approach certitude, the moral principle would be threatened from another direction: fear of divine punishment (and, therefore, hope for divine reward) would so overpower the human being that, even though transgression might be avoided, that would occur in mere conformity to the law, and thus lack any moral worth. "As long as human nature remains as it is, human conduct would thus be changed into mere mechanism in which, as in a puppet show, everything would *gesticulate* well but there would be *no life* in the figures."[41] With humans reduced to mere puppets that act on the basis of inclination rather than free, rational self-legislation, all human dignity and worth would be lost. Once again, Kant's God must hang between life and death, be not so alive as to terrify, nor so dead as to cause the abandonment of hope; God must remain a specter, suspended between life and death, being and nonbeing.

III

If Kant's God is a spectral God, then Kant's religion, a religion *within the limits of reason alone,* must be a spectral religion. Not quite the lived, determinate religion of history, religion within the limits of reason alone nevertheless mirrors determinate religion (Christianity, at least); it functions as a kind of simulacrum of Christianity that nevertheless has as its goal the death of determinate religion. Religion is therefore perpetually in a state of *passing over,* a passing over directly tied to its function as a *vehicle* for morality.

If religion is ultimately meant to consolidate morality, to bridge the chasm between the demand for happiness that attends humanity as sensible and the demands of the moral law that attend humanity as rational, there nevertheless remains the significant problem that what goes by the name of religion—for which Kant uses the word "faith," reserving the designation "religion" for the religion of pure reason—only very rarely seems to promote the moral vocation. In fact, the various determinate, historical faiths seem to get matters precisely backwards. While God remains a dispenser of reward and punishment, such reward and punishment is not dispensed on the basis of one's moral worth, but on the basis of any number of arbitrary statutes that are supposed to please God and yet have no connection to morality. The philosopher has no choice but to wage war against historical faith, a war that aims not at its total destruction—for historical faith can prove useful as a vehicle for the promotion of the religion of reason—but at its submission and transformation into genuinely ethical religion. This war against determinate faiths is a war of interpretation. Kant's *Religion* represents both a profound reinterpretation of scripture and an argument for the rights of the philosopher as interpreter, for the ascendency of the philosopher's interpretation over that of the scholar or theologian.

In *The Conflict of the Faculties,* a text that provides a sort of after-the-fact blueprint for the *Religion,* Kant specifies four hermeneutic principles with which the philosophical interpreter of scripture is to approach the biblical texts. Principle I states: "If a scriptural text contains certain *theoretical* teachings which are proclaimed sacred but which *transcend* all rational concepts (even moral ones), it *may* be interpreted in the interests of practical reason; but if it contains statements that contradict practical reason, it *must* be interpreted in the interests of practical reason."[42] In other words, the only dogmas of an ecclesiastical faith that may be *left alone* by the philosophical interpreter are those that are entirely irrelevant to morality; however, the exegete may nevertheless supply such an interpretation if he so chooses.

Principle II states: "With regard to scriptural teachings that we can know only by revelation, faith is not in itself *meritorious,* and lack of such faith, and even doubt opposed to it, in itself involves no *guilt.* The only thing that matters in religion is *deeds,* and this final aim and, accordingly, a meaning appropriate to it, must be attributed to every biblical dogma."[43] What one finds in this principle is a very decisive stand taken against one particular dogma, that of salvation through faith alone. The notion that God is pleased with anything other than moral action, and would reward someone on such a basis, runs entirely counter to the notion of God produced by practical reason. Therefore, the philosophical interpreter of scripture must neutralize any passage that suggests or supports this dogma.

Principle III states: "Actions must be presented as issuing from the human being's own use of his moral powers, not as an effect [resulting] from the influence of an external, higher cause by whose activity the human being is passively healed. The interpretation of scriptural texts which, taken literally, seem to contain the latter view must therefore be deliberately directed toward making them consistent with the former view."[44] Here, Kant rejects the notion that a human being can only become pleasing to God through God's own divine influence and initiative, and must himself wait passively for such assistance. Kant's rejection of grace, however, is not entirely wholesale, as the fourth principle will show. The point, however, is that for an action to count as a moral one, it must be within the power of the human being to perform such action, independently of divine influence, and any biblical passage which suggests otherwise must be neutralized by the philosophical exegete.

Finally, Principle IV reads: "If the human being's own deeds are not sufficient to justify him before his conscience (as it judges him strictly), reason is entitled to adopt on faith a supernatural supplement to fill what is lacking to his justification (though not to specify in what this consists)."[45] Here Kant specifies what idea of grace a human being is allowed to adopt, even though, strictly speaking, one cannot determine whether such a doctrine is true, given that it touches on matters that transcend human knowledge. The idea here is simple enough: assuming that the human being has, at some point in his life, failed to be a moral person (and hence failed to be pleasing to God), then this constitutes a sin for which the human is unable to atone. Assuming this person has undergone a moral conversion to the good, his conscience may nevertheless judge him displeasing to God on account of this past moral failing. Indeed, his conscience may cause him to despair of the possibility of ever becoming pleasing to God on this account, a despair that may in fact undermine his pursuit of moral perfection. Therefore, Kant allows the possibility of a divine grace that would consist in nothing other than the forgiveness of past misdeeds, assuming, of course, that the human has undergone the revolution in moral disposition that would make him worthy of such forgiveness. The key difference between this justifying grace and the prevenient grace rejected in the third principle is that justifying grace depends upon the human being *making himself* worthy of receiving it, whereas prevenient grace comes prior to and is independent of any moral exertion on the part of the human being.

What is most fascinating about these principles taken as a whole is that Kant shows little concern for what the biblical text *actually says*. His position on the merits of faith versus works, for example, or that of prevenient grace, is determined prior to and independently of the biblical position on those matters. The philosophical interpretation of scripture involves the accommodation, and even willful misreading, of those texts that run counter to the moral principle as Kant determines it; and Kant is hardly bashful about this. How can he justify such a fast and loose approach?

Kant has two answers to this question. The first is that the biblical theologian does this very thing with the biblical texts all the time:

> It seems to violate outright the highest rule of exegesis that reason feels entitled to interpret the text in a way it finds consistent with its own principles, even when it is confronted with a text where no other meaning can be ascribed to the sacred author, as what he actually intended by his words, than one which contradicts reason: [in other words], that we should not interpret the text literally, unless we are willing to charge it with error.—Yet this is what has always happened, with the approval of the most eminent theologians. In their interpretation of scriptural texts which literally contradict our rational concept of God's nature and will, biblical theologians have long made it their rule that what is expressed in human terms must be *interpreted* in a sense worthy of God. By this they quite clearly confess that in matters of religion reason is the highest interpreter of the scriptures.—They follow this rule with regard to St. Paul's teaching on predestination, which clearly shows that his personal view must have been that human beings are predestined in the strictest sense of the term. Although a major Protestant church, following him, adopting this teaching into its creed, a great part of that church later abandoned the doctrine or, as far as possible, changed its meaning, because reason finds that predestination cannot be reconciled with its own teachings on freedom and the imputation of action, and so with the whole of morality.[46]

However true Kant's claim may be, this *tu quoque* argument is hardly enough to establish the validity of his method. Rather, Kant's method finds its ground, such as it is, in the idea that ecclesiastical faith is a "vehicle" for the transmission of moral faith. "Reason does, it is true, claim to interpret dogma, in so far as it is the vehicle of religious faith. But since the value of dogma is only that of a means to religion as its final end, could such a claim be more legitimate?"[47] Since ecclesiastical faith has value only as a means to the end of religious faith (morality), then any interpretation which reads a moral meaning into a non-moral or immoral biblical text or church dogma is in fact putting that text or dogma to the very use for which it is ultimately intended.

If Kant's hermeneutic principles rest upon the subordination of ecclesiastical faith as a vehicle for the transmission of the pure moral faith, then how, one may ask, does Kant justify such subordination in the first place? Kant seems to assume it rather than argue for it in the *Conflict,* which may be explained in part by the fact that the understanding of religion as a "vehicle" was not uncommon in Kant's time. While G. E. Lessing does not use that word, he expresses a very similar conception of religion in "The Education of the Human Race" (1777–80). As Walter Jaeschke notes in *Reason in Religion,* the use of the word "vehicle" (*Vehikel*) in Kant's time was shaped by its pharmacological usage: the "vehicle" denotes the neutral substance that acts as a carrier of the active ingredient.[48] This raises the question, of course, of whether ecclesiastical faith is truly a "neutral" substance, or whether it does in fact counteract the "active ingredient" (the moral principle); the answer is that the entire philosophical thrust of Kant's texts on religion points to the poisonous nature of this so-called neutral element, even if, in another register, Kant continues to insist upon the efficacy of Christianity as a vehicle for genuine religious faith.

Kant's hermeneutic principles as outlined in the *Conflict* bear witness to his awareness that determinate religion is indeed no innocuous transmitter of the moral principle, but a poison that must be neutralized. Practical reason determines *in advance of* any engagement with the biblical texts which kinds of ideas are acceptable and which are not, and the hermeneutic imperative is to re-interpret the text such that it accords with the principles of practical reason by any means necessary, which is to say, even if blatant violence is done to the plain meaning of the text. This, of course, is nothing other than *allegorization.* In the *Religion,* Kant writes:

> We shall also find that this is how all types of faith—ancient and new, some written down in holy books—have always been treated, and that rational and thoughtful teachers of the people have kept on interpreting them until, gradually, they brought them, as regards their essential content, in agreement with the universal principles of moral faith. The moral philosophers among the Greeks and, later, among the Romans, did exactly the same with their legends concerning the gods. They knew in the end how to interpret even the coarsest polytheism as just a symbolic representation of the properties of the one divine being; and how to invest all sorts of depraved actions, and even the wild yet beautiful fancies of their poets, with a mystical meaning that brought popular faith (which it would never have been advisable to destroy, for the result might have been perhaps an atheism even more dangerous to the state) close to a moral doctrine intelligible to all human beings and alone beneficial.[49]

Here Kant justifies the liberties he takes with scripture precisely through recourse to the prevalence of allegory in all faiths.

Kant's attempt to maintain a strict delineation between dogmatic faith and rational religion, and to contain the moral dangers of dogmatic faith, will be the focus of Derrida's reading of Kant's *Religion.* Derrida discusses this in terms of Kant's attempt to eliminate the "fetish" from religion, a gesture that, for Derrida, is constitutive of philosophy of religion as such; whether this fetish is ultimately eliminable from Kant's philosophy of religion, or indeed any philosophy of religion, is, as we will now see, a central question.

2

Parergonality and Fetishism: Deconstructing Kant's *Religion*

I

Derrida's "Faith and Knowledge" consists of 52 numbered sections, the first 26 of which constitute the first part of the text, which is entitled "Italics." This portion of the text is italicized, and is indeed the "Italic" portion of the text, which is to say the address Derrida delivered at the seminar on the island of Capri, Italy, in 1994. The second and non-italicized portion of the text, sections 27–52, is entitled "Post-scriptum," and was added for the published version. The topic of this seminar, whose participants included Gianni Vattimo and Hans-Georg Gadamer, was "religion" and the question of the "return of the religious."

It is interesting that Derrida chose not to integrate the remarks he delivered at the seminar with the remarks added later on for the published version, but rather chose to publish them side by side as two separate, albeit consecutively numbered, parts. This is no doubt to emphasize the location and date on which the remarks were delivered, as well as to keep in view the addressees of his remarks (i.e., the seminar participants); Derrida will frequently draw attention to these three elements (date, location, addressee) throughout the text. But why is the context so significant?

One important reason is that Derrida privileges the question of "pragmatics" in this text. He notes that any attempt to "take measure" of the question "What is religion?" would have to incorporate several programs of investigation. The first program consists in an etymological examination of the word "religion," which provides an initial point of orientation, even if it "never provides a law and only provides material for thinking on the condition that it allows itself to be thought as well."[1] The second program consists in the "search for historico-semantical **filiations** or **genealogies** [. . .] with which the meaning of the word [religion] is put to the test of historical transformations and of institutional structures." The third program involves an analysis concerned with the "pragmatic and functional effects" of "religion"; such an analysis, which would be "more structural and also more political," "would not hesitate to investigate the usages or applications of the lexical resources, where, in the face of new regularities, of unusual recurrences, of unprecedented contexts, discourse liberates words and meaning from all archaic memory and from all supposed origins." After delineating these three programs (etymological, genealogical, and pragmatic), Derrida suggests that, in Capri, the last type ought to dominate; without excluding the other forms of analysis, the seminar should "privilege the signs of what in the world, *today*, singularizes the use of the word 'religion' as well as experience of 'religion' associated with the word, there where no memory and no history could suffice to announce or gather it, at least not at first sight."[2]

The pragmatic question, then, of what is happening with the word "religion" *today* dates the text, links it to a particular place and context. And Derrida will himself date the text, not only at the end of the "Postscriptum" ("Laguna, 26 April 1995"), but also within the main body of the text: "*Yesterday (yes, yesterday, truly, just a few days ago), there was the massacre of Hebron at the Tomb of the Patriarchs, a place held in common and symbolic trench of the religions called 'Abrahamic.'*"[3] Derrida is here referring to the murder of 29 Muslim worshippers by Baruch Goldstein on February 25, 1994. This way of dating his remarks within the text points ahead to the questions of religious violence, terrorism, fundamentalism, and "radical evil" with which this text will be concerned.

The location of the seminar is significant as well, since, as Derrida argues, the question of Rome and the Latin provenance of the word "religion" is central to any interrogation of its meaning.

> *We are not far from Rome, but are no longer in Rome. Here we are literally isolated for two days, insulated on the heights of Capri, in the difference between the Roman and the Italic, the latter potentially symbolizing everything that can incline—at a certain remove from the Roman in general. To think 'religion' is to think the 'Roman.' This can be done neither in Rome nor too far from Rome. A chance or necessity for recalling the history of something like 'religion': everything done or said* in its name *ought to keep the critical memory of this appellation. European, it was first of all Latin.*[4]

The Latinity of "religion" will become an important issue in "Faith and Knowledge." Derrida will refer to the hegemony of Christianity in its connection with "tele-technoscientific capitalism" by the term "globalatinization" (*mondialatinisation*).

However, it is Derrida's repeated reference to his addressees, the participants in the seminar, which bears most directly on the significance of Kant in this text:

> *Let us also remember what, rightly or wrongly, I hold provisionally to be evident: that, whatever our relation to religion may be, and to this or that religion, we are not priests bound by a ministry, nor theologians, nor qualified, competent representatives of religion, nor enemies of religion as such, in the sense that certain so-called Enlightenment philosophers are thought to have been. But we also share, it seems to me, something else—let us designate it cautiously—an unreserved taste, if not an unconditional preference, for what, in politics, is called republican democracy as a universalizable model, binding philosophy to the public 'cause', to the* res publica, *to 'public-ness', once again to the light of day, once again to the 'lights' of the Enlightenment* <aux Lumières>, *once again to the enlightened virtue of public space, emancipating it from all external power (non-lay, non-secular), for example from religious dogmatism, orthodoxy or authority (that is, from a certain rule of the* doxa *or of belief, which, however, does not mean from all faith).*[5]

Here Derrida is delineating the perspective from which the question of religion is being asked within the seminar: the perspective of philosophers with a preference for the Enlightenment (and not the antireligious kind, which immediately places them closer to the *Aufklärung* of Kant than the *Lumières* of Voltaire) and with a distaste for religious dogmatism, orthodoxy, and authority. It is thus not surprising that Derrida should go on to refer to their task as a "transposition" of the Kantian gesture: "[. . .] *we shall doubtless attempt to transpose, here and now, the circumspect and suspensive attitude, a certain* epoché *that consists—rightly or wrongly, for the issue is serious—in thinking religion or making it appear 'within the limits of reason alone.'*"[6]

The terms of this transposition, however, remain to be understood, as the Kantian gesture of thinking "religion within the limits of religion alone" will not necessarily be one unified, self-identical gesture. Derrida no doubt indicates this when he asks, "*What of this 'Kantian' gesture today? What would a book be like today which, like Kant's, is entitled,* Religion within the Limits of Reason Alone*?*,"[7] suggestively placing "Kantian" in quotation marks. We must ask, then, which "Kant" Derrida is attempting to transpose.

II

If it is indeed the case that Derrida's project in "Faith and Knowledge" consists in transposing the Kantian gesture of thinking religion within the limits of reason alone, it remains to be seen in what, precisely, Kant's gesture consists for Derrida. Above all, it consists in Kant's belief that "*only the Christian religion will have been a 'moral' religion,*" a "*strange proposition, but which must be taken as seriously as possible in each of its premises.*"[8]

> *Are we ready to measure without flinching the implications and consequences of this Kantian thesis? The latter seems strong, simple and dizzying: the Christian religion would be the only truly 'moral' religion; a mission would thus be reserved exclusively for it and for it alone: that of liberating a 'reflecting faith'. It necessarily follows therefore that pure morality and Christianity are indissociable in their essence and in their concept. If there is no Christianity without pure morality, it is because Christian revelation teaches us something essential about the very idea of morality. From this it follows that the very idea of a morality that is pure but non-Christian would be absurd; it would exceed both understanding and reason, it would be a contradiction in terms. The unconditional universality of the categorical imperative is evangelical. The moral law inscribes itself at the bottom of our hearts like a memory of the Passion. When it addresses us, it either speaks the idiom of the Christian—or is silent.*[9]

Derrida's meaning here is clear enough; it would be easy to demonstrate that, for Kant, Christianity is the sole moral religion. Derrida goes on to suggest something that is perhaps less obviously a feature of Kant's philosophy of religion. He argues that Kant's thesis that Christianity is the sole moral religion is at the same time a thesis concerning the "death of God":

> *In the definition of 'reflecting faith' and of what binds the idea of pure morality indissolubly to Christian revelation, Kant recurs to the logic of a simple* principle [. . .]*: in order to conduct oneself in a moral manner, one must act as though God did not exist or no longer concerned himself with our salvation. This shows who is moral and who is therefore Christian, assuming that a Christian owes it to himself to be moral: no longer turn towards God at the moment of acting in good faith; act as though God had abandoned us.*[10]

While the moral law, which is antithetical to divine heteronomy, must remain unconditionally binding in the radical absence of God, it is nevertheless the case that Kant holds an essential place for the "idea" of God as that which unites virtue and happiness in the highest good. But God as a postulate of practical reason nevertheless demonstrates, as Derrida argues, a certain "death of God" insofar as it requires a "bracketing" of God's existence and subordination of this existence to the moral principle.[11] In short, morality must be able to function in God's absence, and the idea of God only acquires meaning on the basis of the independent and autonomous moral principle. Derrida continues:

> *In enabling us to think (but also to suspend in theory) the existence of God, the freedom or the immorality of the soul, the union of virtue and of happiness, the concept of 'postulate' of practical reason guarantees this radical dissociation and assumes ultimately rational and philosophical responsibility, the consequence* here in this world, in experience, *of this abandonment.*[12] *Is this not another way of saying that Christianity can only answer to its moral calling and morality, to its Christian calling if it endures in this world, in phenomenal history, the death of God, well beyond the figures of the Passion?*[13]

The moral interpretation of religion, or rather, the complete or nearly complete reduction of religion to the sphere of ethics, which is characteristic not only of Kant but of a major strand of Enlightenment thinking more broadly, involves an experience of the death of God. And it is the alliance of morality and Christianity by way of this experience of the death of God that constitutes the universalizing gesture of Kant and the Enlightenment. Christianity is identical to morality and is thus the only truly universal religion; therefore, in their resistance to the universalizing gesture of Christianity, Judaism and Islam signify a revolt against this death of God:

> *Judaism and Islam would thus be perhaps the last two monotheisms to revolt against everything that, in the Christianizing of our world, signifies the death of God, death in God, two non-pagan monotheisms that do not accept death any more than multiplicity in God (the Passion, the Trinity etc.), two monotheisms still alien enough at the heart of Graeco-Christian, Pagano-Christian Europe, alienating themselves from a Europe that signifies the death of God, by recalling at all costs that 'monotheism' signifies no less faith in the One, and in the living One, than belief in a single God.*[14]

For Kant, however, Judaism and Islam never attain to the status of "true religion" precisely because these "religions" are not based upon moral principles, but upon divine heteronomy. Kant in fact generally reserves the word "religion" for pure moral religion (of which Christianity is, for Kant, the only example). Nevertheless, Kant does posit, as Derrida notes, two families of religion, "*and hence two genealogies of which it still must be asked why they share the same name whether proper or common <noun>* [sic]." These two families are "religion of the cult alone" (*des blossen Cultus*), which seeks God's favor and does not oblige man to become better; and "moral religion," which enjoins man to a good life conducted "*in accordance with the following principle: '"It is not essential and hence not necessary for everyone to know what God does or has done for his salvation," but it is essential to know what* man himself must do *in order to become worthy of this assistance.'*"[15]

Kant states this principle in the "General Remark" appended to Part I of the *Religion;* each of the four parts of the *Religion* concludes with a "General Remark." These are of particular interest to Derrida because Kant defines them as "parerga," which do not belong to "religion within the limits of reason" but border upon it. Derrida comments on these parerga not only in "Faith and Knowledge," but also in the "Parergon" essay in 1978's *The Truth in Painting.*

Kant explains the function of these parerga at the end of the first "General Remark":

> This General Remark is the first of four which are appended, one to each Part of this writing, and which could bear the labels 1) Of effects of Grace; 2) Miracles; 3) Mysteries; and 4) Means of Grace.—These are, as it were, *parerga* to religion within the boundaries of pure reason; they do not belong within it yet border on it. Reason, conscious of its impotence to satisfy its moral needs, extends itself to extravagant ideas which might make up for this lack, though it is not suited to this enlarged domain. Reason does not contest the possibility or actuality of the objects of these ideas; it just cannot incorporate them into its maxims of thought and action. And if in the inscrutable field of the supernatural there is something more than it can bring to its understanding, which may however be necessary to make up for its moral impotence, reason even counts on this something being made available to its good will even if uncognized, with a faith which (with respect to the possibility of this something) we might call *reflective,* since the *dogmatic* faith which announces itself to be a *knowledge* appears to reason dishonest or impudent: for to remove difficulties that obstruct what stands firm on its own (practically), when these difficulties touch upon transcendent questions, is only a secondary occupation (*parergon*).[16]

Kant makes a distinction between rational religion, which belongs to pure philosophical morals, and material (or historical) religion, which, insofar as it concerns revelation and dogma, belongs outside the realm of a philosophical morality. And yet, according to Kant, there is an overlap between these two domains, such that the true content of Christian revelation is identical with philosophical ethics. It is the hermeneutic enterprise of interpreting Christian revelation through the lens of this philosophical ethics that yields what Kant calls "religion within the limits of reason alone." The main body of Kant's text, then, consists of an explication of this "religion within the limits of reason alone," which is ultimately identical to a pure philosophical ethics; what takes place in the "General Remarks," however, does not belong within this philosophical ethics or "religion of reason," but neither does it belong wholly outside of it. Why then are these "General Remarks" necessary, if they are not a part of religion within the limits of reason? They are necessary because of a *lack* within reason itself: "Reason, conscious of its impotence to satisfy its moral needs, extends itself to extravagant ideas which might make up for this lack, though it is not suited to this enlarged domain." This lack causes reason to go beyond its own proper jurisdiction into the "enlarged domain" that concerns "transcendent questions." The problem, however, is that these transcendent ideas—grace, miracles, and mysteries, about which man can have no knowledge—threaten the moral principle:

> As regards the disadvantages that result from these ideas (which are also *morally* transcendent), when we wish to introduce them into religion, their effects, in the order of the four classes mentioned above, are as follows: (1) supposed inner experience (effects of grace), *enthusiasm;* (2) alleged outer experiences (miracles), *superstition;* (3) presumed enlightenment of the understanding with respect to the supernatural (mysteries), *illumination,* the delusion of the initiates; (4) adventurous attempts at influencing the supernatural (means of grace), *thaumaturgy,* sheer aberrations of a reason that has strayed beyond its limits, indeed for a supposed moral aim (one pleasing to God).[17]

As Kant says, it is not a matter of denying the existence of grace, mysteries, or miracles, since reason itself cannot "contest the possibility or actuality of the objects of these ideas," precisely because these are not possible objects of experience; but neither can reason attest to their actuality. What reason cannot do, above all, is incorporate these ideas into its moral maxims, precisely because they tend to pervert morality and lead to the "aberrations of reason" that Kant classifies as enthusiasm, superstition, belief in illumination, and belief in thaumaturgy.

It is important to note the *quasi-transcendental* structure at work here: the parerga to the religion of reason are necessary because they fill a lack within reason itself; in this sense, the parerga function as a condition of possibility of rational religion. And yet, precisely because these parerga extend reason beyond its proper domain, they compromise the purity of rational religion, and thereby act as the condition of impossibility of a pure moral religion. It is this quasi-transcendental structure that acts as the deconstructive lever for Derrida's reading of Kant's *Religion,* disrupting the distinction that Kant attempts to preserve between rational and historical religion. In *Truth and Painting,* Derrida makes this explicit:

> What is translated as "secondary task" is *Nebengeschäfte:* incidental business or bustle, activity or operation which comes *beside* or *against.* The *parergon* inscribes something which comes as an extra, *exterior* to the proper field (here that of pure reason and of *Religion within the Limits of Reason Alone*) but whose transcendent exteriority comes to play, abut onto, brush against, rub, press against the limit itself and intervene in the inside only to the extent that the inside is lacking. It is lacking *in* something and it is lacking *from itself.* Because reason is "conscious of its impotence to satisfy its moral need," it has recourse to the *parergon,* to grace, to mystery, to miracles. It needs the supplementary work. This additive, to be sure, is threatening. Its use is critical. It involves a risk and exacts a price the theory of which is elaborated. To each *parergon* of *Religion* there is a corresponding damage, a detriment (*Nachteil*) and the four classes of dangers will correspond to the four types of *parergon.*[18]

In addition to the quasi-transcendental structure of the *parerga,* the other key feature of this first General Remark is Kant's employment of the term "reflective faith." Kant says the following about the opposition between reflective and dogmatic faith:

> And if in the inscrutable field of the supernatural there is something more than it can bring to its understanding, which may however be necessary to make up for its moral impotence, reason even counts on this something being made available to its good will even if uncognized, with a faith which (with respect to the possibility of this something) we might call *reflective,* since the *dogmatic* faith which announces itself to be a *knowledge* appears to reason dishonest or impudent: for to remove difficulties that obstruct what stands firm on its own (practically), when these secondary difficulties touch on transcendent questions, is only a secondary occupation (*parergon*).[19]

When reason, on account of its own impotence, is forced to believe in something that transcends its proper jurisdiction, this faith is *reflective* as opposed to *dogmatic* precisely because it does not involve a claim to *knowledge* concerning what reason cannot know. Everything that will transpire in the course of the General Remarks, then, happens under the banner of reflective faith. And Kant asserts that this is a "secondary occupation," or *parergon,* precisely because it involves providing a solution for difficulties concerning transcendent questions, even though the thing that these difficulties obstruct "stands firm on its own (practically)."

What Kant refers to as "reflective faith" involves, by his own admission, a transgression of the boundaries of reason, precisely because it touches upon "transcendent questions." "Dogmatic faith" transgresses the bounds of reason as well. The only difference between these two types of faith is that dogmatic faith "announces itself to be a *knowledge*," while reflective faith is guilty of no such dishonesty. But the question arises: if reflective faith transgresses the boundaries of reason, is it not exposing itself to the constant danger of passing over into a dogmatic faith? How, if at all, can this danger be contained?

Though Kant attempts to keep separate the domains of dogmatic faith and reason, it is nevertheless the case that reason's internal lack in fact necessitates faith, and therefore can no longer be strictly opposed to faith. Indeed, it is the irreducibility of a certain "faith" that Derrida will attempt to "transpose" in "Faith and Knowledge," articulating a notion of faith that is essential to reason. But this will not come in the form of a dialectical resolution of the antinomy between faith and reason. This notion of faith will still be "parergonal," no longer in the sense of "secondary," but in the sense that it exposes reason to a certain danger. But just like the parergonal structure that Kant articulates, faith will also be the condition of possibility of reason, and, therefore, will be a *necessary* danger.

Proof that Derrida's "Faith and Knowledge" represents a transposition of this Kantian problematic lies in the fact that Derrida says, concerning the concept of reflective faith, that its "*possibility might well open the space of our discussion,*"[20] and then comments a few pages later:

> *This definition of* reflecting faith *appears in the first of the four* Parerga *added at the end of each section of* Religion within the Limits of Reason Alone. *These* Parerga *are not integral parts of the book; they 'do not belong within' 'religion in the limits of pure reason', they 'border upon' it. I stress this for reasons that are in part theo-topological, even theo-architectonic: these* Parerga *situate perhaps the fringe where we might be able, today, to inscribe our reflections.*[21]

"Reflective faith" is a term that provides a banner under which the attempt to transpose the Kantian gesture can take place, not because it aims at universality in the manner of "rational faith," but because it deconstructs the universalizing gesture of a supposedly universal and rational faith identical to Christianity, and yet also seeks to resist dogmatism, orthodoxy, and everything that Kant classifies as "dogmatic faith." "Reflective faith," then, effectively deconstructs the pretense of establishing a pure religion of reason as well as the desire to maintain the purity of this rational faith against the contamination of statutory religion.

Of course, Derrida's strategy in employing this notion of reflective faith is not exactly identical to Kant's. Kant wishes to isolate a pure rational faith, and envisions the disappearance of statutory religion—which, he claims, is only a vehicle for moral religion—as the *telos* of religion. Hence Kant anticipates the triumph of a pure moral faith. While Kant does recognize the difficulties involved in maintaining the demarcation between rational and statutory religion—difficulties that necessitate the parerga and reflective faith—he nevertheless attempts to reduce these difficulties to the status of an accident. But what if statutory religion is not an accident that befalls moral religion? What if the resurgence of dogmatism is a *structural possibility* that conditions the very existence of moral religion? This would call into question the teleological triumph of moral religion, the identification of Christianity as the one universal and purely moral religion, and indeed the very distinction between moral and statutory religion.

If rational religion constitutes the essence of religion, the "thing itself" of religion, Kant's purpose will be, ultimately, to keep the thing itself safe from any substitution by false claimants (statutory religions). And it is the belief that one can maintain a strict delimitation between the thing itself and its substitutes that Derrida will call the "classical logic of the fetish." Moreover, Derrida will define the "philosophy of religion" precisely in terms of the attempt to banish the fetish from religion. A deconstruction of this classical logic of the fetish and of its Kantian manifestation will amount, then, to a deconstruction of the philosophy of religion itself.

III

Among Derrida's unpublished materials are eight lectures for a 1972–73 seminar entitled "*Religion et philosophie.*" Some of the material from these lectures was eventually published, along with material from other seminars, in *Glas* in 1974. Specifically, the portion of these lectures published in *Glas* is the section devoted to Hegel's philosophy of religion. But this seminar also contains substantive analyses of Kant, Marx, and Freud not included in *Glas.* The analysis of Kant consists of a detailed reading of Part IV of the *Religion,* and is specifically concerned with Kant's use of the concept of the "fetish."

In these unpublished lecture manuscripts, Derrida focuses on the question of "counterfeit service" to God, which occupies the second half of Part IV of the *Religion.* The important question Kant addresses here can be stated as follows: if Christianity is indeed founded upon pure moral faith, and if the statutory elements of Christianity are strictly subordinated to moral faith, whence comes religious delusion?

The point that Derrida emphasizes in the lecture manuscript[22]—a point that is not formulated against Kant's text, but through it—is that what Kant denounces as religious delusion does not simply involve an empirical or accidental weakness, but is rather a system with its own proper rationality, and is therefore a "perversion" insofar as it is structured and organized, commanded by a rule and the automatization of repetition. For Kant, "religious delusion" consists precisely in deeming "this statutory faith (which is in any case restricted to one people and cannot contain the universal world religion) essential to the service of God in general," and making it "the supreme condition of divine good pleasure toward human beings." Religious delusion is therefore in essence a process of *substitution.* In a footnote to this definition of religious delusion, Kant notes that delusion in general consists in "the mistake of regarding the mere representation of a thing as equivalent to the thing itself"; thus the delusion of "madness" consists in taking a mere representation of the imagination for the "presence of the thing itself, and to value it as such."[23] In the case of religion, delusion consists in the substitution of the statute, which is arbitrary and contingent, for true service to God, which consists only in acting out of respect for the moral law. Acting upon this delusion is what constitutes "counterfeit service" to God.

The locus of religious delusion is the "strange institution" called the church, which, Derrida notes, is never condemned as such by Kant, and yet is nevertheless the primary target of his criticism. What makes the church such a "strange institution," according to Derrida, is that it is entirely resistant, in Kant's discourse, to a number of basic categories. It is neither purely social nor purely political, because it is an ethical community that nevertheless requires a statutory element. Moreover, it is both historical and ahistorical, and therefore neither completely historical nor completely ahistorical. It is ahistorical insofar as it represents the moral principle that, since it is rational, properly speaking it has no history; and yet, insofar as it is statutory, it is fundamentally historical, linked to concrete institutions.

Kant's uneasiness with regard to the church consists in the fact that saving religion from delusion requires removing from it every specificity and determination. If it is the church and religious representation that give rise to religious delusion, or at least make possible the ever-present risk of delusion, then it is only morality that can save religion, by means of the following principle: "*Apart from a good life-conduct, anything which the human being supposes that he can do to become well-pleasing to God is mere religious delusion and counterfeit service of God.*"[24] The church can only avoid folly by submitting itself to the purely moral end. But what, Derrida asks, constitutes the proper function of the church if it is submitted to pure morality? Kant cannot do without the church, Derrida says, precisely because the system of visible representation is required to compensate for man's irreducible moral insufficiency, an insufficiency that derives from his finitude, his combination of rational and sensible natures. This is Kant's double-bind: if a moral religion is necessary on account of man's finitude (the fact that the moral law is not his sole end), and a pure religion nevertheless requires a historical, statutory faith in order to become effectively universal, then the delusion that arises from statutory faith is not merely accidental. The possibility of delusion is a necessary condition for the possibility of an effectively universal religion of reason.

If the possibility of religious delusion cannot be foreclosed, then neither can the possibility of "fetishism." Kant's usage of this word represents a significant mutation in the meaning of this then newly coined term.[25] Rather than designating "primitive" or "savage" religious practice, as it did for Kant's contemporaries, fetishism is for Kant a characteristic of the church itself. Kant writes:

> The veneration of mighty invisible beings, which was wrung from the helpless human being because of the fear naturally rooted in the consciousness of his powerlessness, did not immediately begin with a religion but with the servile worship of God (or gods) which, whenever it received a certain public and legal form, became a *temple service;* and it became an *ecclesiastical service* only after the moral culture of human beings gradually came to be associated with these laws: at the foundation of both lies a historical faith, until we finally begin to regard them as provisional, and we begin to see in them the symbolic representation and the means of furtherance of a pure faith of religion.[26]

Fetishism does not belong to the period before the church in which invisible beings were venerated out of fear, but only arises when the moral principle enters into this worship. Thus Kant defines fetishism exactly as he defined religious delusion:

> Whoever therefore gives precedence to the observance of statutory laws, requiring a revelation as necessary to religion, not indeed merely as a means to the moral disposition but as the objective condition for becoming well-pleasing to God directly, and whoever places the striving for a good life-conduct behind the historical faith (whereas the latter, as something which can only be well-pleasing to God *conditionally,* ought to be directed to the former, which alone pleases God *absolutely*)—whoever does this transforms the service of God into mere *fetishism;* he

> engages in a counterfeit service, which sets back all the work leading to true religion.[27]

This represents a modification of the usage of "fetishism," insofar as it is a feature of the church rather than primitive religion. Nevertheless, Kant's usage preserves the structure of the normal usage: the fetishist venerates his fetish as if it were the invisible power itself, attributing value to the substitute rather than the thing itself. So, too, Kant's fetishist substitutes the observance of statutory laws for a moral disposition, believing the former to be well-pleasing to God.

It is Kant's project in the *Religion* to eliminate the fetish (religious delusion) and replace it with the thing itself of pure moral religion. And yet, if religious delusion is the result of religious representation, which itself is ultimately necessitated by human finitude, then the possibility of the fetish is not foreclosable. Pure moral religion, rigorously demarcated from statutory religion, never takes place as such. Religion threatens morality as much as it promotes it. Once again, reason's insufficiency requires that it go beyond its proper boundaries; yet this transgression exposes reason to the threat of an immoral faith. For Derrida, then, Kant's discourse ultimately belongs to the "classical logic of the fetish," to which Derrida opposes a general undecidability of the fetish—or what he calls, based on his reading of Freud's classic 1927 paper on fetishism, the "argument of the *girdle*."[28]

According to Derrida, Freud, like Kant, operates according to the "classical logic of the fetish," which is to say, according to the belief that one can rigorously dissociate the fetish as substitute from the thing itself. Freud writes:

> In all the cases the meaning and purpose of the fetish turned out under analysis to be the same. It revealed itself so unequivocally and seemed to me so categorical that I should expect the same solution in all cases of fetishism. When I now disclose that the fetish is a penis-substitute, I shall certainly arouse disappointment; so I hasten to add that it is not a substitute for any chance penis, but for a particular quite special penis that had been extremely important in early childhood but was afterwards lost. That is to say: it should normally have been given up, but the purpose of the fetish is to preserve it from being lost. To put it plainly: the fetish is a substitute for the woman's (mother's) phallus which the little boy once believed in and does not wish to forgo—we know why.[29]

Freud's analysis here is well known. The boy refuses to acknowledge that his mother in fact has no penis, for if a woman can be castrated, then he can be castrated as well; so a compromise is struck in the unconscious. The woman still has a penis in the boy's psychic reality, although the penis has been replaced by something else. "Something else has taken its place, has been appointed its successor, so to speak, and now absorbs all the interest which formerly belonged to the penis." This substitute then serves as a "token of triumph over the threat of castration and a safeguard against it"; but so too does it enable the fetishist to overcome his aversion (present in every fetishist, according to Freud) to the female genitals, thereby saving the fetishist "from being a homosexual by endowing women with the attribute which makes them acceptable as sexual objects."[30] As for the substitutes themselves, they are usually, says Freud, the last impression received before the traumatic experience memorialized by the fetish:

> Thus the foot or the shoe owes its attraction as a fetish, or part of it, to the circumstance that the inquisitive boy used to peer up the woman's legs towards her genitals. Velvet and fur reproduce—as has long been suspected—the sight of the pubic hair which ought to have revealed the longed-for penis; the underlinen so often adopted as a fetish reproduces the scene of undressing, the last moment in which the woman could still be regarded as phallic.[31]

The process thus outlined, one of substitution of a representation for the thing itself, in this case, the substitution of the fetish object for the phallus, could be called the classic logic of the fetish.

Derrida focuses on the penultimate paragraph of the "Fetishism" paper, where this logic of the fetish begins to unravel. This is where Freud comes to the question of the girdle. Freud writes:

> In very subtle cases the fetish itself has become the vehicle both of denying and of asseverating the fact of castration. This was exemplified in the case of a man whose fetish was a suspensory belt which can also be worn as bathing drawers; this piece of clothing covers the genitals and altogether conceals the difference between them. The analysis showed that it could mean that a woman is castrated, and it even allows of a supposition that a man may be castrated, for all these possibilities could equally well be hidden beneath the belt; its forerunner in childhood had been the fig-leaf seen on a statue. Naturally, a fetish of this kind constructed out of two opposing ideas is capable of great tenacity.[32]

Whereas according to the classic logic of the fetish, the relationship between the substitute and the thing itself was a decidable and stable relation, in the case of this more "tenacious" fetish, the relation between substitute and thing itself becomes undecidable. As Geoffrey Bennington comments: "The description of the 'classical' case is then, as it were, itself already a disavowal of the 'subtle' one, an attempt to stabilize the meaning of the fetish by making it the substitute of some one thing, whereas the general logic of substitution is one in which the best or most 'durable' fetish (such as the girdle) is radically substitutive, and to that extent no longer really a substitute at all."[33] Thus Freud, on the one hand, attempts to arrest and stabilize the meaning of the fetish, whereas in fact it rests on a fundamental undecidability. Derrida comments: "The construction of the fetish rests *at once* on the denial and on the affirmation (*Behauptung*), the assertion or the assumption of castration. This at-once, the in-the-same-stroke, the *du-même-coup* of the two contraries [. . .] prohibits cutting through to a decision within the undecidable."[34] Derrida's analysis of the classic logic of the fetish is essential, as we will see in a moment, to his understanding of Kant's philosophy of religion.

In the unpublished portions of Derrida's seminar as well as in *Glas* itself, one finds a repeated juxtaposition of Kant and Freud. This juxtaposition is prompted by, on the one hand, Freud's own claim to have discovered the origin of morality and thereby discovered the true meaning of the categorical imperative, and, on the other, Kant's own belief that his ethics is founded upon pure rationality freed from all pathology. In the Preface to *Totem and Taboo,* Freud comments that the analysis he offers concerning the taboo is "put forward as an assured and exhaustive attempt at the solution of the problem," whereas his psychoanalytic analysis of the totem is provisional; the different degree of confidence in the analysis is related to the fact that, unlike totemism, taboos still exist among us: "Though expressed in a negative form and directed towards another subject-matter, they do not differ in their psychological nature from Kant's 'categorical imperative', which operates in a compulsive fashion and rejects any conscious motives."[35] Yet the relationship between the taboo and the categorical imperative is not one of simple analogy; the analysis of the taboo provides the means for penetrating to the very origin of the categorical imperative, and therefore, to the origin of morality:

> It may begin to dawn on us that the taboos of the savage Polynesians are after all not so remote from us as we are inclined to think at first, that the moral and conventional prohibitions by which we ourselves are governed may have some essential relationship with these primitive taboos and that an explanation of taboo might throw a light upon the obscure origin of our own 'categorical imperative.'[36]

Such an interpretation of the categorical imperative would no doubt be unacceptable for Kant, for whom the moral principle not only is not psychological, but does not even have anything to do with "man" at all. While not seeking to provide a psychoanalytic reading of Kant, Derrida is nevertheless interested in the way in which Kant's texts open themselves to such a reading through their inability to wholly exclude the pathological.[37]

It is thus not surprising that in the lecture manuscript, Derrida will comment at length on the way in which the notion of being "well-pleasing to God" opens itself to a psychoanalytic investigation. Why, Derrida asks, must one please God? Throughout Kant's *Religion*, it is repeatedly stated that it is necessary to be well-pleasing to God. But this pleasure, which belongs as much to ethics (pure rational religion) as it does to historical religion, is never interrogated as such. What is the nature of this pleasure, since one has no direct access to God? How can an "auto-nomic" and "auto-affecting" operation (submitting oneself to the moral law) be pleasing to God? This is a question, Derrida says, that could spark the beginning of a psychoanalytic investigation that gives a rigorous account of this Kantian system and interrogates the "interiorization" or "incorporation" of God (the father) into a psychic organization in which the father is given as absent and unexperienceable, and yet commands unconditionally. What does it mean to wish to please an absolutely absent being so imperiously demanding pleasure, a pleasure, moreover, that can only be given to him by one who renounces for himself all empirical pleasure and all sensible motivation (i.e., the hypothetical imperatives which do *not* please God)? The pleasure of the dead father as categorical imperative, Derrida suggests, could constitute an interpretation and translation of Kant's condemnation of the system of religious delusion.

In *Glas*, Derrida places Kant in an imaginary dialogue not only with Freud, who wishes to get to the "thing itself" of Kant's ethics, to the true origin of morality, but also with Hegel, who, in his turn, accuses Kant of fetishism. Indeed, the attempt to expose the fetish constitutes, for Derrida, the basic gesture of the "philosophy of religion":

> To found *or* to destroy religion [. . .] always comes down to wanting to reduce fetishism. Fetishism, to form against itself the unanimity of founders and destroyers, must indeed somewhere constitute the opposing unity: the unveiling of the column, the erection of the thing itself, the rejection [*rejet*] of the substitute. [. . .] As long as fetishism will be criticized [. . .] will the economy of metaphysics, the philosophy-of-religion, have been tampered with?[38]

"Philosophy of religion" is thus linked with the critique of fetishism as the "rejection of the substitute" and the "erection of the thing itself." For Derrida, this process is indeed at work in Kant's *Religion*, though Kant's text resists the clear demarcation of substitute (statutory faith) and thing itself (pure moral religion). Thus there is in the *Religion,* as in Freud's text, an undecidability of the fetish.

Derrida notes that for Kant as well as Hegel, "the teleological horizon of 'true and unique religion' is the disappearance of the fetish";[39] and yet, Hegel and Kant differ as to precisely what constitutes the thing itself of religion. Derrida says that according to Hegel:

> The (Kantian) precept according to which "we can know nothing of God" is a prejudice of the time with which one must break if one wants to inaugurate a philosophy of religion. Hegel never questions that this philosophy of religion must be Christian. But he draws from it a diametrically opposed conclusion: if in piety the question is pleasing God the Father and taking pleasure in the law (Kant), is striving for perfection to that end, how would that be possible if we were enclosed in the phenomenon and left God beyond knowledge (theoretical knowledge, what Hegel does not want to distinguish here from the practical relation)? According to the formalizable law of a chiasm(us), Hegel in sum reproaches Kant with being unfaithful to reason and to Christianity, just as Kant reproaches those who believe they know God (that will have been the case with Hegel) with degrading religion to religious folly, to the delirium of arrogance, or to fetishism. "This [Kantian] standpoint [. . .] [is] opposed to the whole nature of the Christian religion." Revelation is revelation. A revealed religion is a religion in which God reveals himself. He does not hide himself, does not hold himself back or in reserve, does not guard himself in it. The Christian religion is true, because it is the religion of truth, manifestation, and revelation.[40]

This "law of chiasmus" signifies the mutual accusations of fetishism that Kant and Hegel hurl at each other in this fictitious dialogue. Hegel accuses Kant of fetishism for worshipping a God who never reveals himself as such, a notion of God antipathetic to Christianity, which is the highest and most complete religion precisely because it is the religion of *revelation.* Kant, on the other hand, accuses Hegel of fetishism precisely because he thinks he can know God speculatively, claiming access to the idea of God through a path other than that of practical reason. It must be said that even though Derrida is speaking in the above passage in Hegel's voice, it is certainly not the case that Derrida sides with Hegel in his war against Kant.[41] Indeed, one of the main points of Derrida's reading of Hegel in *Glas* is that Hegel himself harbors a certain fetish within his philosophy of religion.[42]

In short, Hegel's accusation is that Kant is fundamentally "Jewish" in that "he believes in a jealous, envious God, who hides and guards his

Da" (the *Da* of his *Dasein*).[43] But Hegel is not the only one criticizing Kant here. Freud is present as well, reducing the categorical imperative to the taboo imposed on the son by the dead father. Derrida allows Kant to respond to this Freudian critique: "'Every genealogy of morals described by psychoanalysis [. . .] is valid perhaps in a field of phenomenal empiricalness, for particular mores, for this determinate culture, for the empiric relations between sensible fathers and sons, for finite psychological determinations, for nonuniversal, nontrue religions, for idolatries and fetishisms.'" But this is not the case for true morality and pure religion, which break with all sensible representation and heteronomy. Thus Freud is guilty of a "'crude analogism'" when he suggests that the taboo does not differ from the categorical imperative.[44]

Hegel, for his part, reenters the dialogue, claiming that Freud was right to see in Kant's ethics and philosophy of religion "finitude, sensible representation, psychologism, fetishism, the relations of jealousy between the hidden, invisible father and the impotent son," since Kant fails to reach the thought of the infinite and, therefore, true religion (which would not be open, for Hegel, to the same psychoanalytic critique). Kant then criticizes Hegel for his own complicity with religious delusion and fetishism, "effacement of Christianity, infidelity, neopaganism," precisely because he believes himself able to attain a speculative knowledge of God.[45]

Derrida's purpose here is not to intervene or mediate in the debate in any way, but rather to show that the attempt to isolate the fetish and demarcate the substitute and the thing itself produces a "merry-go-round" and a "vicious circle" that cannot be closed off or put to an end as such.[46] But this raises a question: how does one think religion without reproducing this fundamental gesture of philosophy of religion, without reproducing the classical logic of the fetish? Derrida will not pretend to provide, in "Faith and Knowledge," a philosophy of religion that escapes this aporia. And this is precisely why Derrida inscribes his reflections under the term "reflective faith." For Derrida, it is "reflective faith" that disrupts Kant's intended demarcation between moral faith (the thing itself) and dogmatic faith (the substitute), thus precluding the foreclosure of the fetish. Derrida's reading of the *Religion* shows that his use of "reflective faith" is specifically meant to signal that such a foreclosure of the fetish is impossible, and that philosophy will never manage to neutralize its threat. But before turning to Derrida's redeployment of "reflective faith" in his attempt to transpose Kant's gesture of thinking religion "within the limits of reason alone," I will turn to Derrida's reading of Kant's ethics—a crucial step for understanding "Faith and Knowledge."

3

Derrida and Kantian Ethics

I

Kant is not the first name that comes to mind when one thinks of Derrida's writings on ethics; Levinas has been, with good reason, the name most associated with Derrida in this connection. As such, the place of Kant in Derrida's writings on ethics is frequently glossed over. And yet one fails to understand what Derrida says about ethics if Kant's place in Derrida's texts is ignored. Kant is as important a point of reference for Derrida as Levinas; in fact, the central aporia of ethics is located precisely at the intersection of *justice* and *law*, ideas for which Derrida metonymically employs the names "Levinas" and "Kant" respectively.

One common way of interpreting Derrida's relationship to Levinas is to insist that Derrida's "Violence and Metaphysics" does not represent a *critique* of Levinas, but a "double-handed" reading that affirms the basic thrust of Levinasian thought, while nevertheless showing that, in *Totality and Infinity,* Levinas's attempt to think an alterity irreducible to the same ("being" or "ontology," in the language of Levinas) involves a necessary complicity with the very ontology he seeks to exceed. This constitutes a necessary corrective to Levinas's work which, so the argument goes, Levinas took into account in his next major work, *Otherwise than Being,* in which he makes a distinction between the Saying (*le Dire*) and the Said (*le Dit*) that acknowledges the gap between a thinking that exceeds ontology and the inevitably compromising language in which this thought is expressed. The ultimate stake of this argument, found in Robert Bernasconi's influential essay "The Trace of Levinas in Derrida,"[1] is a vindication of Levinas against Derrida's seemingly critical reading. Simon Critchley then puts this argument to the further use of demonstrating a homology between Derrida and Levinas, claiming that one can therefore speak of an "ethics of deconstruction," with the proviso that this ethics is a Levinasian one.

On the one hand, it would be impossible to deny an affinity between Derrida and Levinas. Each finds his philosophical point of departure in phenomenology, each is concerned with the effacement of alterity in the philosophical tradition, and each has no doubt exerted an influence upon the other's work, whether in the form of the "trace" in Derrida or the distinction between Saying and Said in Levinas. Nevertheless, it would be imprudent to downplay the significance of Derrida's deconstructive reading of Levinas, precisely because this reading exposes fundamental difficulties in Levinas's determination of ethics, difficulties that have major consequences for the ability to speak of an "ethics of deconstruction."

In "Violence and Metaphysics," Derrida notes that Levinas's ethical project manages to be "at once profoundly faithful to Kant" "and implicitly anti-Kantian." The proximity lies in the fact that Levinas's ethics involves an immediate respect for the other, and the distance in the fact that this respect "does not pass through the neutral element of the universal." The search for a truly universal moral principle sets Kant's entire practical philosophy in motion. For Kant, this universality precludes any pathological action from having ethical value, precisely because pathology is not universal. And as Derrida notes, the element of universality prevents respect for the other from collapsing into such "empirical and pathological immediacy." Levinas's ethics, however, is an ethics of the singular obligation to the other, and resists recourse to, or mediation by, the concept of universality, since such universality necessarily limits the singular responsibility to the other. For Levinas, respect for the other is not mediated by respect for the law. Consequently, Derrida poses the question, without providing an answer, of how respect and the other in Levinas's ethics would escape empirical and pathological immediacy.[2] This is a truly Kantian question that already points to the difficulty of any ethics that would eschew the element of universality. But it is not simply that universality is required to avoid a pathological immediacy; in fact, there is no access to the otherness of the other that does not proceed according to some universal element. A particularly forceful example of this is found in the pages that Derrida devotes to Levinas's denunciation of the fifth of Husserl's *Cartesian Meditations*.

One of Levinas's fundamental disagreements with Husserl is the reduction of the other to a phenomenon of the ego through the process of analogical appresentation in the *Cartesian Meditations*. According to Husserl, the other would be known on the basis of an essentially inferential process, wherein the other is recognized on the basis of its similarity with the ego. According to Levinas, such a derivation of the other constitutes a breach of the absolute alterity of the other, reducing the other to an alter ego. Derrida strongly objects to Levinas's reading of Husserl, claiming that according to the "most manifest and most massively incontestable meaning" of the fifth of the *Cartesian Meditations*,

> Husserl's most central affirmation concerns the *irreducibly mediate* nature of the intentionality aiming at the other as other. It is evident,

> by an essential, absolute, and definitive self-evidence that the other as transcendental other (other absolute origin and other zero point in the orientation of the world), can never be given to me in an original way and in person, but only through analogical appresentation. The necessary reference to analogical appresentation, far from signifying an analogical and assimilatory reduction of the other to the same, confirms and respects separation, the unsurpassable necessity of (nonobjective) mediation. If I did not approach the other by way of analogical appresentation, if I attained to the other immediately and originally, silently, in communion with the other's own experience, the other would cease to be other. Contrary to appearances, the theme of appresentative transposition translates the recognition of the radical separation of the absolute origins, the relationship of absolved absolutes and nonviolent respect for the secret: the opposition of victorious assimilation.[3]

Thus the fact that for Husserl the other can only be accessed mediately through the process of analogical appresentation does not reduce the other to the same, but in fact acknowledges and respects the alterity of the other. To put it another way, the other can only be accessed on the basis of an analogy with the same if it is to be recognized as other at all. Without any such analogy, one forfeits all right to speak of the absolutely other. And indeed, this is perhaps the most fundamental feature of Derrida's reading of Levinas: by attempting to maintain a thinking of absolute alterity that breaks completely with the "same," Levinas remains at a loss for language adequate to this alterity. While Husserl gives himself the "right" to speak of the other by "acknowledging in this infinitely other *as such* (appearing as such) the status of an intentional modification of the ego in general," Levinas "*in fact* speaks of the infinitely other, but by refusing to acknowledge an intentional modification of the ego—which would be a violent and totalitarian act for him—he deprives himself of the very foundation and possibility of his own language."[4]

Beyond the difficulty of the representation of a radical alterity free from all complicity with ontology, there lies the further insurmountable difficulty generated by Levinas's attempt to determine the ethical relation as one of an infinite and unilateral responsibility for the other. If one were to grant Levinas this definition of "ethics" (and Derrida himself will not *wholly* deny it, as I will show), the difficulty arises that there is never in fact only *one* other to whom I am responsible, but a multitude of others, a point that Derrida makes in the *Gift of Death:* "[W]hat binds me thus in my singularity to the absolute singularity of the other immediately propels me into the space of absolute sacrifice. There are also others, an infinite number of them, the innumerable generality of others to whom

I should be bound by the same responsibility, a general and universal responsibility."[5] Martin Hägglund notes quite correctly that the net result of Derrida's insight here is that there is a "necessity of discrimination," of mediation between the needs of a multitude of others to whom one is infinitely responsible.[6]

Levinas himself was responsive to Derrida's criticisms, and this type of criticism, centered around the problem of multiple others, is to a certain extent answered by way of Levinas's notion of the "third." If infinite responsibility to the other is a relationship between *two,* then the third interrupts this relationship by being present as another other. This third other also demands my responsibility and therefore elicits a need for the comparison between these competing singularities. Yet, as Derrida argues in *Adieu: To Emmanuel Levinas,* this "third" is not secondary to the face to face of the ethical relationship, but imposes itself immediately: "This move out of purely ethical responsibility, this interruption of ethical immediacy, is itself immediate. The third does not wait." And this is not simply because there are always already other others, but also because the immediacy of the face to face encounter lends itself to a certain violence: "For the absence of the third would threaten with violence the purity of ethics in the absolute immediacy of the face to face with the unique."[7] Indeed, an infinite responsibility can very well result in a kind of exploitative ethical violence. Hägglund summarizes this point effectively: "It is thus quite crucial for Levinas that the subordination to a tyrant [. . .] can be rigorously distinguished from the subordination to an ethical other. But it is precisely the possibility of such a distinction between the 'good' other and the 'bad' other that the deconstructive analysis calls into question."[8]

The immediacy of the third and, therefore, the immediacy of calculation and mediation between competing claims (which, for Levinas, gives rise to the question of justice and philosophical discourse) entail an effacement of the supposed priority of the face-to-face encounter. Derrida writes:

> Though Levinas never puts it in these terms, I will risk pointing out the necessity of this *double-bind* in what follows from the axioms established or recalled by Levinas: if the face to face with the unique engages the infinite ethics of my responsibility for the other in a sort of *oath before the letter,* an unconditional respect or fidelity, then the ineluctable emergence of the third, and, with it, of justice, would signal an initial perjury [*parjure*]. Silent, passive, painful, but inevitable, such perjury is not accidental and secondary, but is as originary as the experience of the face. Justice would begin with this perjury. (Or at least justice as law; even if

> justice remains transcendent or heterogeneous to law, these two concepts must not be dissociated: justice *demands* law, and law does not wait any more than does the illeity of the third in the face. When Levinas says "justice," we are also authorized to hear "law," it seems to me. Law [*droit*] would begin with such a perjury; it would betray ethical uprightness [*droiture*].)[9]

Far from an antecedent purity of the ethical relationship, Derrida posits an originary perjury in the name of the ineluctability of the third that, by calling for mediation and calculation, violates the ethical as Levinas defines it. There is no ethics outside of "law," which is to say, outside of a principle of universality capable of mediating these competing claims and putting an end to the violence of the face-to-face encounter. In other words, ethics in the Levinasian sense is *stricto sensu* impossible without an ethics of the Kantian type, though "ethics" in the Kantian sense represents a violation of ethics in the Levinasian sense. This is precisely the double-bind of Levinasian ethics. It is clear, then, that for Derrida, ethics in the Levinasian sense is impossible, precisely because what makes such an ethics possible simultaneously destroys it. And by extension, one cannot rightly claim that there is an ethics of deconstruction, if this ethics is taken in the Levinasian sense.

Despite the fact that there is no deconstructive ethics in the Levinasian sense (or any other sense, as will become clear), Ernesto Laclau notes that in Derrida there is sometimes an "ambiguity" between the descriptive and prescriptive levels of analysis, an ambiguity which makes possible an "illegitimate transition": "The illegitimate transition is to think that from the impossibility of a presence closed in itself, from an 'ontological' condition in which the openness to the event, to the heterogeneous, to the radically other is constitutive, some kind of ethical injunction to be responsible and to keep oneself open to the heterogeneity of the other necessarily follows."[10] This ambiguity is precisely related to the fact that, even though there is no such thing as an unconditional ethical demand in the Levinasian sense, Derrida nevertheless frequently makes use of this thought of the unconditional, enabling an assimilation between the "unconditional" in Derrida and "infinite responsibility" in Levinas. But if, as Laclau notes, deconstruction itself does not give rise to any prescriptive ethical injunctions, then whence comes this thought of the unconditional in Derrida?

This ambiguity is resolvable, provided one understands the twofold source of the interpretive difficulty. It stems first from a failure to distinguish, on the one hand, "deconstruction" from "deconstructive reading," and on the other, "deconstructive reading" from "*Derrida's* deconstructive reading." Second, this difficulty derives from the fact that a number of essentially "descriptive" concepts that Derrida employs are given names that carry an ethical and even religious resonance, thereby making possible the confusion between descriptive and prescriptive levels. It is important to know, however, why these names are chosen to represent the particular structures they designate. Moreover, it is important to follow the aporetic or quasi-transcendental nature of these structures themselves. Attentiveness to these details will reveal that, while in certain respects, these structures are similar to the things customarily designated by the same names ("faith" and "the messianic," for example), in other respects they are radically heterogeneous to them, as will become clear further on.

Derrida often said that deconstruction is not something that one *does to* a text, that there is no subject or agent of deconstruction, but rather that deconstruction is a process that is always already at work in a text;[11] if this is the case, then the problem with claiming that there is an ethics of deconstruction becomes readily apparent: there can be no ethical injunction associated with what is always already taking place. Deconstruction, understood in this way, remains radically heterogeneous to any ethical injunction. However, when we move from deconstruction as such to a "deconstructive reading," the question of "ethics" becomes relevant, because now there is something like an *agent* of deconstruction, however minimal and self-effacing this agent might be. While a deconstructive reading may very well only be following the deconstruction already at work in the text, it nevertheless remains that *someone* is performing this reading, someone presumably possessing a particular motivation for performing this kind of reading of this particular text. It is possible, then, to defend the claim that there is an ethical injunction associated with deconstructive reading only if we understand this ethical injunction as one that does not derive from deconstruction as such, even when this injunction motivates a deconstructive reading. Consequently, "respect for the other" can attach itself to a deconstructive discourse without being derived from deconstruction as such. And of course a deconstructive reading can be undertaken out of any number of motivations that are not Levinasian. Any such motivation, however, will only be a contingent product of a particular interest, which is to say that such a motivation is, to use Laclau's Gramscian terminology, a "hegemonic" one. This is not a negative judgment or a denunciation of any such motivation on account of its contingency. It is simply to say that there is no ethico-political decision that is not an essentially violent one—a conclusion totally in keeping with "deconstruction." Deconstruction itself does not sanction any one particular ethico-political decision, though such a decision might motivate a particular deconstructive reading.

Next, there is the question of *Derrida* and of the particular ethico-political decisions that motivate *his* particular deconstructive readings. Derrida will speak of a passion for justice that motivates deconstruction; but this passion can only be the passion of Derrida himself. Not every deconstructive reading is inspired by a similar passion. It would be absurd to pretend that there is an exclusive, inevitable link between deconstruction and Derrida's particular ethico-political stance, a stance that Derrida summarizes in "Faith and Knowledge" when, addressing the other scholars gathered at a seminar in Capri, he says that they all

> *share, it seems to me, something else—let us designate it cautiously—an unreserved taste, if not an unconditional preference, for what, in politics, is called republican democracy as a universalizable model, binding philosophy to the public 'cause', to the* res publica, *to 'public-ness', once again to the light of day, once again to the 'lights' of the Enlightenment* [aux Lumières], *once again to the enlightened virtue of public space, emancipating it from all external power (non-lay, non-secular), for example from religious dogmatism, orthodoxy or authority (that is, from a certain rule of the* doxa *or of belief, which, however, does not mean from all faith).*[12]

While democracy is Derrida's avowed preference, is not the inevitable outcome of deconstruction, as Laclau has argued:

> Precisely because of the undecidability inherent in constitutive openness, ethico-political moves different from or even opposite to a democracy 'to come' can be made—for instance, since there is ultimate undecidability and, as a result, no immanent tendency of the structure to closure and full presence, to sustain that closure has to be *artificially* brought about from the outside. In that way a case for totalitarianism can be presented starting from deconstructionist premisses. Of course, the totalitarian argument would be as much a *non sequitur* as the argument for democracy: either direction is equally possible given the situation of structural undecidability.[13]

Thus, the direction in which one can proceed with a deconstructive insight is not limited to the direction taken by Derrida himself; Laclau correctly notes that "with any deconstruction worthy of the name, there is a plurality of directions in which one can move."[14] Therefore, where Derrida does indicate some kind of ethico-political engagement, it is important not to identify this engagement with deconstruction in the first sense, which, as something always already at work in the text, cannot be said to give birth to an ethics or politics as such.

When translated into ethico-political terms, the lack of pure presence signifies not simply the inability of any totality to be closed in on itself, but also the unattainability of any non-violent universality. Universality remains an empty signifier,[15] betrayed, as it were, by any interest that happens to insert itself in its place. This insight certainly follows from a rigorously deconstructive thinking; yet the question is what one *does* with such an insight, how the irreducible violence against the other translates into political action. While deconstruction does not prescribe anything in the way of ethico-political action, it nevertheless remains that a deconstructive reading can be undertaken in the name of an ethico-political program. For example, if one values pluralism and respect for the other in a Levinasian vein (despite the fact that, as we have seen, any transcription into the political necessarily betrays the supposed purity of Levinasian ethics), then one could argue for a political system in which the hegemony and violence of any particular interest is limited in its pursuit of universality by competing interests that are also able to assert their claims in the political realm, i.e., some form of democracy. This is a legitimate political goal, but one that, as Derrida recognizes, is auto-deconstructing, for two primary reasons. First, a universal culture of singularities is aporetic and unattainable, since difference can never be entirely absorbed into a non-violent universality; second, the value of "pluralism" is not itself universal, since difference can be tolerated only when those who are different are willing to tolerate difference as well. Pluralism therefore can never practically be radicalized to the point where all differences are respected as such without limitation.[16] This is why Derrida speaks not of "democracy," but of a "democracy to come," not as a future democracy that is on its way, that someday might arrive, but as a democracy that is precisely impossible, the object of a desire or passion for the impossible. *Deconstruction* does not desire the impossible; *Derrida* desires the impossible. In emphasizing the impossibility of the democracy to come, Derrida is no doubt exercising a sort of critical vigilance, a hyper-reflexivity of discourse, since he is exposing the inevitable violence of any actually existing democracy or democratic institution.

Derrida is often hyper-reflexive, however, to the point where such concepts lose all practicability. This is why his thought seems somehow politically useless when it is at its most vigilant. His vigilance against the violence inherent in any ethico-political determination can result, therefore, in a sort of political paralysis. Richard Rorty voices just such an objection to deconstruction (which he clearly mistakenly equates with "Derrida") in a piece entitled "Remarks on Deconstruction and Pragmatism." In this essay, Rorty makes a distinction he himself describes as "crude" between philosophers like Mill, Dewey, and Rawls, "whose work fulfills primarily public purposes, and those whose work fulfills primarily private purposes."[17] It is as "private self-creation" that Rorty reads Derrida's texts, and he takes issue with the "particularly Levinasian strains in his thought." Rorty claims to be "unable to connect Levinas's pathos of the infinite with ethics or politics," which he sees rather as "a matter of reaching accommodation between competing interests, and as something to be deliberated about in banal, familiar terms." At the end of this piece, Rorty concludes:

> I see romantic and utopian hopes of the sort developed in "The Politics of Friendship" as a contribution to Derrida's private self-fashioning, and thus to that of some of his readers [. . .]. Politics, as I see it, is a matter of pragmatic, short-term reforms and compromises—compromises which must, in a democratic society, be proposed and defended in terms much less esoteric than those in which we overcome the metaphysics of presence.[18]

This sentiment has been echoed by Fiona Jenkins, who, in a long footnote to her article "Gestures Beyond Tolerance," writes that one of her reservations concerning Derrida's notion of unconditional hospitality concerns "the risk that the ethical moment of absolute justice is here separated from a political-pragmatic order of right in a gesture repeating the separation of the humanitarian impulse to help all others from the political calculation which delineates the practical limits of this project."[19]

Yet these are not objections that come at Derrida from the outside; the aporia between respect for the singularity of the other and the question of the competing interests of multiple others is precisely the aporia with which Derrida is concerned. While Derrida clearly recognizes that a pure respect for the singularity of the other is *stricto sensu* impossible, he nevertheless maintains that it is not possible to distinguish a greater violence from a lesser violence without a thought of infinite respect for the singularity of the other (which Derrida's terms "hospitality"). Derrida writes:

> We often forget that it is in the name of unconditional hospitality, the kind that makes meaningful any reception of foreigners, that we should try to determine the *best* conditions, namely particular legal limits, and especially any particular implementation of the laws. This is always forgotten, by definition, when it comes to xenophobia: but it can also be forgotten in the name of a certain "pragmatism" and "realism." [Such overly pragmatist] tactics [. . .] could well lose more than their soul: they could lose the calculated benefit.[20]

In other words, for Derrida, one can only think a greater or lesser violence if one is animated by the "impossible" thought of a pure hospitality. Again: "Without at least the thought of this pure and unconditional hospitality, of hospitality *itself,* we would have no concept of hospitality in general and would not even be able to determine any rules for conditional hospitality (with its rituals, its legal status, its norms, its national or international conventions)."[21] Derrida's thought, then, involves a type of ethico-political commitment that is Levinasian, even though Derrida has rightly deconstructed the idea that there is any such thing as ethics in the Levinasian sense.

Derrida's writings on ethics, then, complicate and indeed preclude any attempt to formulate an "ethics of deconstruction." However, as I have argued, while deconstruction itself—that is to say, deconstruction as something that is *always already at work*—remains inhospitable to ethics, this does not mean that one finds no prescriptive injunction at work in *Derrida's deconstructive readings.* Any attempt to completely empty Derrida's texts of all concrete ethico-political commitments can only result in a serious misconstrual of these texts. Such misconstrual is at work in Martin Hägglund's *Radical Atheism: Derrida and the Time of Life.*

Hägglund, whose attempt to disjoin Derrida and Levinas is a necessary corrective to the various attempts to formulate an ethics of deconstruction, nevertheless himself disavows those places in Derrida's text where this notion of an infinite or unconditional responsibility is given a positive meaning as a desire for the impossible. Concerning unconditional hospitality, Hägglund writes:

> As distinct from the ethics of unconditional hospitality he deconstructs, Derrida's notion of unconditional hospitality designates the exposure to the unpredictable, which can always be violent and to which one cannot know in advance how one should relate. The "hospitality" to otherness is unconditional *not* because it is ideal or ethical as such, but because one is necessarily susceptible to violent visitations. Even the most conditional hospitality is thus unconditionally hospitable to that which may ruin it.[22]

Hägglund is certainly correct that Derrida distinguishes between an unconditional hospitality of visitation and a conditional hospitality of invitation, and he is right to stress the danger to which any openness to the other exposes us; indeed, this is why Derrida links such openness to the other to the possibility of radical evil. However, this is not the only, or even the primary, way in which Derrida uses the word "unconditional." It is impossible to deny that for Derrida, the unconditional is not rejected simply because it is "impossible" as such; rather, this "impossibility" also signifies, as I will demonstrate, a productive and motivating force. Hägglund's desire to disjoin Derrida and Levinas is no doubt motivated by the desire to show that deconstruction cannot produce any kind of ethical injunction, Levinasian or otherwise; but Derrida's positive use of the notion of the unconditional does not mean that there is an "ethics of deconstruction." It only means that Derrida's deconstructive readings are motivated by a certain ethico-political stance that itself remains, as Derrida was well aware, unavoidably open to further deconstruction.

In fact, Hägglund is very much aware that Derrida's use of the word "unconditional" does often involve a kind of prescriptive injunction. In a lengthy footnote in *Radical Atheism,* Hägglund concedes that there are places in Derrida's writings in which an unconditional openness to the other is positively valorized. He cites one example and implies that others exist. But the rest of this chapter will bear witness to the fact that Derrida's positive use of the idea of the unconditional runs much deeper than some scant examples. Hägglund calls such instances "occasional inconsistencies" on Derrida's part; such a positive valorization of unconditional openness to the other, he claims, "is untenable given the logic of deconstruction."[23] But one hardly needs to point out the absurdity of making an argument about Derrida's writings while altogether dismissing passages that do not fit with one's conception of what Derrida *should* say.[24] It is naïve to think that Derrida's writing (or anyone else's, for that matter) could ever be devoid of an ethico-political stance, or that deconstructive reading could ever take place independent of any injunction that prescribes this very deconstruction.

II

The essential point I have developed so far is that if, for Derrida, an unconditional responsibility to the other is always already betrayed by the "third," which is to say, that ethics requires the mediation of the "law," then Derrida's thinking is linked to that of a certain Kant, for whom the unconditional (categorical) imperative is always mediated through the universality of the law. Derrida's thinking, the thinking that animates his own deconstructive interventions in the ethical tradition, has a decidedly Kantian resonance. However, just as Derrida's thinking retains a trace of Levinas even as he subjects Levinas to an intense deconstructive reading in the name of a type of Kantianism, so too is Kant in turn the object of a deconstructive reading in the name of a certain Levinasianism.

In an interview with Gerald Graff published in *Limited Inc,* Derrida recalls the fact that in a number of his writings he has made appeal to the notion of the unconditional, and comments:

> Now, the very least that can be said of unconditionality (a word that I use not by accident to recall the character of the categorical imperative in its Kantian form) is that it is independent of every determinate context, even of the determination of a context in general. It announces itself as such only in the *opening* of context. Not that it is simply present (existent) elsewhere, outside of all context; rather, it intervenes in the determination of a context from its very inception, and from an injunction, a law, a responsibility that transcends this or that determination of a given context. Following this, what remains is to articulate this unconditionality with the determinate (Kant would say hypothetical) conditions of this or that context; and this is the moment of strategies, of rhetorics, of ethics, and of politics.[25]

Derrida is drawing an explicit link between this notion of the unconditional and the Kantian categorical imperative. Moreover, the aporia consisting of the need to reconcile the unconditional responsibility for the other with the competing demands of other others, and therefore, the need to reconcile this unconditionality with a pragmatics, is framed in terms of the need to articulate this unconditional imperative within the demands of *context,* which he characterizes, again using Kantian language, in terms of "hypothetical imperatives."

It is important to keep in mind here that Derrida is evoking a certain proximity with Kant; but this proximity, just like Derrida's proximity to Levinas, should not be mistaken for identification. Derrida goes on to explain why it is that he does not, in face of this proximity, characterize his thinking in Kantian terms:

> This unconditionality also defines the injunction that prescribes deconstructing. Why have I always hesitated to characterize it in Kantian terms, for example, or more generally in ethical or political terms, when that would have been so easy and would have enabled me to avoid so much criticism, itself all too facile as well? Because such characterizations seemed to me essentially associated with philosophemes that themselves call for deconstructive questions. Through these difficulties, another language and other thoughts seek to make their way. This language and these thoughts, which are also new responsibilities, arouse in me a respect which, whatever the cost, I neither can nor will compromise.[26]

It will become clear further on, in connection with another of Derrida's names for the unconditional, "justice," why Derrida says that this unconditionality defines the "injunction that prescribes deconstructing." But it is important to note that Derrida resists assimilation with Kantian ethics precisely because there are, in Kant, elements that call for deconstruction; and the "facile" use of Kantian language would demonstrate a lack of fidelity to this thinking of the unconditional that animates Derrida's deconstruction in the first place. Thus, the task of my reading of Derrida's engagements with Kant's ethics consists not simply in articulating Derrida's "positive" relationship to the Kantian categorical imperative, but also in examining his deconstruction of philosophemes bound to this Kantian framework.

III

In "Passions: 'An Oblique Offering,'" Derrida writes that both politeness and friendship involve a certain ritualized decorum; and yet, one would hesitate to say that an act was truly friendly or polite if it was done simply out of a sense of duty to abide by these rituals. While conformity to the rules of friendship or politeness is necessary, it is not a sufficient condition for the determination of friendship or politeness. Consequently, friendship and politeness involve both rules and norms that govern their proper execution as well as an injunction to go beyond the mere letter of the ritual, an injunction to "invention without rule." This would be the case not only for politeness and friendship, but for all normative concepts. "We thus have here a rule—and this rule is recurrent, structural, general, that is to say, each time singular and exemplary—which commands action of such a sort that one not act simply by conformity to the normative rule but not even, by virtue of the said rule, out of respect for it."[27] What seems to go wrong, in such cases, is that the relationship to the other is mediated entirely through the general rules of politeness or friendship, and no attention is paid to the other in his singularity. "Invention without rule," then, involves attentiveness to the singularity of the other without mediation by the universal (the general laws or rules of friendship or politeness).

Yet this injunction to "invent without rule" immediately produces a paradox: would not this second-order duty to transgress this duty (i.e., not act simply out of duty) generate yet another duty to transgress this second-order duty as well? This "being-double of duty," then, the duty to transgress duty, "hollows itself out in an infinite abyss."[28] We are faced, then, as Derrida says, with the question

> of knowing whether and up to what point one can rely on [the concept of duty], on what it structures in the order of culture, of morality, of politics, of law, and even of economy (especially as to the relation between debt and duty); that is to say, whether and up to what point one can trust what the concept of duty lays down for all responsible discourse about responsible decisions, for all discourse, all logic, all rhetoric *of* responsibility.[29]

The concept of duty, of course, is central to Kant's determination of the moral law. Accordingly, Derrida proceeds, in the footnotes to "Passions," to interrogate the Kantian notion of duty.

In the Preface to the *Groundwork of the Metaphysics of Morals,* Kant comments on the nature and purpose of his investigation of morality:

> Since my aim here is directed properly to moral philosophy, I limit the question proposed only to this: is it not thought to be of the utmost necessity to work out for once a pure moral philosophy, completely cleansed of everything that may be only empirical and that belongs to anthropology? For, that there must be such a philosophy is clear of itself from the common idea of duty and of morals. Everyone must grant that a law, if it is to hold morally, that is, as a ground of an obligation, must carry with it absolute necessity; that, for example, the command "thou shalt not lie" does not hold only for human beings, as if other rational beings did not have to heed it, and so with all other moral laws properly so called; that, therefore, the ground of obligation here must not be sought in the nature of the human being or in the circumstances of the world in which he is placed, but a priori simply in concepts of pure reason; and that any other precept, which is based on principles of mere experience—even if it is universal in a certain respect—insofar as it rests in the least part on empirical grounds, perhaps only in terms of a motive, can indeed be called a practical rule but never a moral law.[30]

This passage provides the fundamental orientation of Kantian ethics. An ethical obligation can only really be an obligation if it is universally binding; and if merely empirical ends determine obligation, this obligation cannot be truly universal, since these ends can vary from person to person. Rather, the moral principle must be rational and a priori. This then leads to the fundamental distinction between categorical imperatives, commands that are unconditional and therefore universal, and hypothetical imperatives, which are conditionally binding, which is to say, binding only if one wants to achieve a particular end. This is why Kant refers to hypothetical imperatives as "practical rules" but not "moral laws."

It is thus no surprise that, in his attempt to ground ethics on truly universal principles, Kant would determine the "goodness" of an action to lie not in the ends that are attained thereby, but rather in the will itself. The opening line of Section I of the *Groundwork* thus reads: "It is impossible to think of anything at all in the world, or indeed even beyond it, that could be considered good without limitation except a **good will.**"[31] Kant says, slightly further on:

> A good will is not good because of what it effects or accomplishes, because of its fitness to attain some proposed end, but only because of its volition, that is, it is good in itself and, regarded for itself, is to be valued incomparably higher than all that could merely be brought about by it in favor of some inclination and indeed, if you will, of the sum of all inclinations. Even if, by a special disfavor of fortune or by the niggardly provision of a stepmotherly nature, this will should wholly lack the capacity to carry out its purpose [. . .] then, like a jewel, it would still shine by itself, as something that has its full worth in itself. Usefulness or fruitlessness can neither add anything to this worth nor take away from it. Its usefulness would be, as it were, only the setting to enable us to handle it more conveniently in ordinary commerce or to attract to it the attention of those who are not yet expert enough, but not to recommend it to experts or to determine its worth.[32]

In these eloquent opening pages of the *Groundwork,* one does not as yet hear an appeal to those austere philosophemes that seem to best characterize Kantian ethics: duty, the categorical imperative, and respect for the law. This is because the argumentative procedure of the *Groundwork* consists in a type of ascent from common, everyday moral cognition to a purely philosophical ethics. Therefore, while it is the good will and *not* duty or respect for the moral law that is the starting point of Kant's ethics, the concepts of duty and moral law will be necessary to explicate philosophically the notion of a good will as the only good "without limitation." Ultimately, Kant will defend what he believes to be the "common-sense" notion of morality, but in a philosophical language. As Nietzsche wryly yet accurately remarks, "Kant wanted to prove, in a way that would dumbfound the common man, that the common man was right: that was the secret of this soul. He wrote against the scholars in support of popular prejudice, but for the scholars and not for the people."[33]

It is important to note the pervasive economic motif that Kant employs in this passage from the *Groundwork.* The worth or value of the good will is not, like any ordinary commodity, linked to its use-value.

In this sense it is like a "jewel": its value is almost completely divorced from any usefulness it might possess. This value, since it is precisely not a use-value, will not attract the attention of those not "expert" enough to see its true value. By "expert," Kant in fact means, paradoxically, "ordinary" moral cognition. Either one is "expert" or one is not, that is, one perceives the "incomparably higher" value of the good will or one does not. The good will is precisely not something that can be demonstrated by a use-value, not simply because it is of a "higher value" than things with a use-value, but because it is of "incomparably" higher value, which is to say, of an entirely different order from the useful. The best that one could do for someone lacking such an "expert" understanding would be to try to explain it in terms of usefulness; but this usefulness would be "only the setting to enable us to handle it more conveniently in ordinary commerce" in order thereby to "attract it to the attention of those who are not yet expert enough." The incomparable value of the good will, then, is divorced from any economy of exchange. I note the economic motif here in part because it is a fundamental way in which Kantian ethics resonates with the notion of the unconditional in Derrida, as discussed above: the good will as the unconditional is that which breaks with all conditionality, all calculation, and all exchange. But Derrida's reading of Kant's ethics will show that there is no way to isolate this unconditional value, that the unconditional is always already contaminated. Just as the jewel only shows itself in the setting that compromises its pure value, so too will the moral principle only be possible on the basis of a certain complicity with the non-moral; to put it another way, ethics is only possible on the basis of a certain structurally necessary, a priori contaminability.

Before coming to Derrida's analysis, however, it is necessary to specify the notion of duty in Kant. If the good will is what has ultimate ethical value, how is it that we can determine what constitutes the action of a good will? If the will is good not because of the particular end that it wills, what does determine whether or not a will is "good"? It is in order to answer this question and explicate this concept of the good will that Kant summons the concept of "duty."

I say that Kant "summons" this concept here precisely because in this first section of the *Groundwork,* Kant is still dealing with common moral cognition, so that what "duty" is does not need to be proven by rational argumentation, because it should be immediately recognized by this moral cognition. After stating that being "beneficent" when possible is a duty, Kant notes that there are some people so "sympathetically attuned" that they are capable of beneficence without any self-interested motive, because they find an "inner satisfaction" in the satisfaction of others. But Kant immediately discounts that such action possesses "moral worth" precisely because the action, though in conformity with duty, is nevertheless performed not out of duty, but out of inclination.[34] It is important to understand this claim correctly. Kant is not denying the possibility that one can act out of duty and yet also experience joy in performing this duty. Rather, he simply says that this example does not lend any specificity to concept of duty because it is unclear, in this case, whether the source of beneficence is inclination or duty. But on the other hand, suppose

> that the mind of this philanthropist were overclouded by his own grief, which extinguished all sympathy with the fate of others, and that while he still had the means to benefit others in distress their troubles did not move him because he had enough to do with his own; and suppose that now, when no longer incited to it by any inclination, he nevertheless tears himself out of this deadly insensibility and does the action without any inclination, simply from duty; then the action first has its genuine moral worth.[35]

This is not to suggest that one is only acting morally when one is cold and indifferent toward others. But this example of one who is otherwise indifferent acting out of duty despite this indifference demonstrates the point that Kant wishes to make: moral worth is located not in any inclination, since inclination is not common to all rational beings (in other words, it belongs to empirical, sensible nature); rather, moral worth is located in acting because it is one's duty to act regardless of one's inclinations. Only action from duty can be a truly universal principle of action and therefore be a candidate for the moral principle.

Having located the value of the good will in acting from duty rather than inclination, Kant is able to specify that "an action from duty has its moral worth *not in the purpose* to be attained by it but in the maxim in accordance with which it is decided upon, and therefore does not depend upon the realization of the object of the action but merely upon the *principle of volition* in accordance with which the action is done without regard for any object of the faculty of desire." The principle of volition, rather than the end attained, is what constitutes the morality of an action. But this leads us to the further question: if it is not the desired end that determines the principle of volition, then what, precisely, determines it? Kant's answer is that "*duty is the necessity of an action from respect for law.*"[36] With all inclination set aside, the only thing left to motivate the will to act in accordance with the law is respect for the moral law itself.

One further point needs to be made before proceeding to Derrida's analysis, namely, that acting out of duty is not characteristic of the good will in general, but of a *finite* good will. As H. J. Paton notes in his commentary on the *Groundwork,* "A will which acts for the sake of duty is a good will; but it must not be supposed that a good will is necessarily one which acts for the sake of duty. On the contrary, a completely good and perfect will would never act for the sake of duty; for in the very idea of duty there is the thought of desires and inclinations to be overcome."[37] It is only a finite will which experiences any inclination to act contrary to the moral law, and therefore, only a finite will which experiences the moral law in the form of a command or an imperative.[38]

The finite will alone is capable of acting contrary to the moral law. But even when this finite will acts in conformity with the moral law, this is not sufficient to determine that action as moral, since there may have been a motive for acting in conformity with the law other than respect for the law. Central to Kant's ethics is the distinction between actions that are done out of (for the sake of) duty, *aus Pflicht,* and actions that are merely in conformity with duty, *pflichtmässig*. It is only the former that can be called truly moral actions; actions that are performed in mere conformity to duty may be *legal,* but are not *moral.* In Chapter 3 of the *Critique of Practical Reason,* Kant writes:

> What is essential to any moral worth of actions is *that the moral law determine the will immediately*. If the determination of the will takes place *conformably* with the moral law but only by means of a feeling, of whatever kind, that has to be supposed in order for the law to become a sufficient determining ground of the will, so that the action is not done *for the sake of the law,* then the action will contain *legality* indeed but not *morality*.[39]

It is this distinction between "out of duty" and "in conformity with duty," morality and legality, spirit and letter, that occupies Derrida's attention in "Passions." Here, Derrida draws attention to something that Kant himself already acknowledges, namely that it is impossible to establish with any certainty whether an action is done for the sake of duty or merely in conformity to duty. In the *Groundwork,* Kant writes:

> In fact, it is absolutely impossible by means of experience to make out with complete certainty a single case in which the maxim of an action otherwise in conformity with duty rested simply on moral grounds and on the representation of one's duty. It is indeed sometimes the case that with the keenest self-examination we find nothing besides

> the moral ground of duty that could have been powerful enough to move us to this or that good action and to so great a sacrifice; but from this it cannot be inferred with certainty that no covert impulse of self-love, under the mere pretense of that idea, was not actually the real determining cause of the will; for we like to flatter ourselves by falsely attributing to ourselves a nobler motive, whereas in fact we can never, even by the most strenuous self-examination, get entirely behind our covert incentives, since, when moral worth is at issue, what counts is not actions, which one sees, but those inner principles of actions that one does not see.[40]

Kant argues in this passage that the determination of whether an action is done *aus Pflicht* or *pflichtmässig* reaches a phenomenal limit; one can see the actions, but not the principles that motivate them. And this holds equally true for the examination of other people and for self-examination, since we are capable of having "covert incentives," motives that act in secret. The problem, then, is the ability of the finite rational being to have a secret that it hides from itself and from others. Derrida comments that, if it is impossible to eliminate the suspicion that the moral subject is harboring a secret, there is "no hope for a rigorous decontamination between 'in conformity with duty' and 'out of pure duty.'"[41]

The point that Derrida makes in this footnote, however, is not simply Kant's point, that there is a phenomenal limit to the ability to distinguish between *aus Pflicht* and *pflichtmässig;* rather, Derrida argues that the contamination of duty here belongs to the very structure of the concept of duty:

> The decontamination is impossible not by virtue of some phenomenal or empirical limit, even if indelible, but precisely because this limit is not empirical; its possibility is linked *structurally* to the possibility of the "out of pure duty." Abolish the possibility of the simulacrum and of external repetition, and you abolish the possibility both of the law and of duty themselves, that is, of their recurrence. Impurity is principally inherent in the purity of duty, i.e., its iterability.[42]

Since duty is linked to the law, and a law can only be a law if it is repeatable over a plurality of instances, the repetition is structurally linked to the law as its very condition of possibility. Moreover, duty is constitutive of a finite rational being and not an infinite one precisely because it is only a finite being who is capable of experiencing the law as "other," which is to say, is capable of *not* acting in accordance with that law. It would be impossible for God to act contrary to the moral law, and as such, God cannot be said to be capable of genuinely moral action precisely because God has no other choice. Consequently, the gap between a finite will and the moral law is the space that makes moral action possible as such. But this gap opens up the possibility of dissimulation, of acting only in conformity with duty rather than out of duty, a possibility that is nevertheless a condition for any "law" whatsoever. Consequently, the fundamental contaminability of *aus Pflicht* and *pflichtmässig* is not an accident that befalls morality but is rather structurally constitutive of the moral principle. Just as the possibility of acting in secret makes moral action possible, so too does it make it impossible to determine whether moral action ever in fact takes place.

IV

Clearly, what Derrida is doing with Kant's ethics here is not refutation; rather, his reading consists of a procedure of drawing out certain implications already present in Kant's texts. The deconstructive reading of Kant's text, however, affects not only the distinction between acting out of duty and acting in conformity to duty, but also Kant's attempt to rigorously exclude the "example" from all ethical thinking.

Acting in conformity to duty and not out of duty essentially involves miming, imitating, or simulating moral action; however, this mimetic iterability is not an accident that befalls the moral law, but a structural necessity. But Kant, in his attempt to maintain the rigor of the *aus Pflicht/pflichtmässig* distinction, must exclude the possibility that one can derive morality from particular examples of moral action. Kant writes:

> Nor could one give worse advice to morality than by wanting to derive it from examples. For, every example of it represented to me must itself first be appraised in accordance with principles of morality, as to whether it is also worthy to serve as an original example, that is, as a model; it can by no means authoritatively provide the concept of morality. Even the Holy One of the Gospel must first be compared with our ideal of moral perfection before he is cognized as such; even he says of himself: why do you call me (whom you see) good? none is good (the archetype of the good) but God only (whom you do not see). But whence have we the concept of God as the highest good? Solely from the *idea* of moral perfection that reason frames a priori and connects inseparably with the concept of a free will.[43]

This passage from the *Groundwork* anticipates Kant's philosophical hermeneutic of religion in *Religion within the Limits of Reason Alone.* Kant makes his argument against the example here by refuting the idea that one can derive morality even from its most perfect example, the "Holy One of the Gospel." But if one cannot derive morality from examples, is there any function for a "moral example"? Kant continues: "Imitation has no place at all in matters of morality, and examples serve only for encouragement, that is, they put beyond doubt the practicability of what the law commands and make intuitive what the practical rule expresses more generally, but they can never justify setting aside their true original, which lies in reason, and guiding oneself by examples."[44]

Examples serve for encouragement, Kant says, because they "put beyond doubt the practicability of what the law commands"; but it should be clear by now that in fact, according to Kant's own analysis, there is never any assurance that a moral action was indeed moral, i.e., performed out of respect for the moral law, without any secret motives. Consequently, no single example can "put beyond doubt" the "practicability of what the law commands"; one can never be sure that a particular example in fact represents a genuine instantiation of the moral law. And as Derrida points out, Kant says a few pages later that one can only investigate how the question of the categorical imperative is *possible,* since "it cannot be made out *by means of any example,* and so empirically, whether there is any such imperative at all, but it is rather to be feared that all imperatives which seem to be categorical may yet in some hidden way be hypothetical."[45] Derrida comments: "This is a most radical claim: no experience can assure us of the 'there is' at this point. God himself therefore cannot serve as an example, and the concept of God as sovereign Good is an idea of reason. It remains that the discourse and the action (the passion) of Christ demonstrates *in an exemplary way,* singularly, par excellence, the inadequacy of the example, the secret of divine invisibility and the sovereignty of reason."[46]

Derrida analyzed the problems associated with imitation and the moral example in *Of Grammatology,* nearly thirty years before the "Passions" essay. There he noted that the problem of the example in Kant is nearly identical in formulation to that in Rousseau's *Emile.*[47] According to Rousseau's pedagogical theory, Derrida writes, "everything begins with imitation and the child learns only by example. Here *imitation is good,* it is more human, it has nothing to do with aping."[48] But even this good imitation entails risk. Derrida adds:

> But this good imitation already carries within itself the premises of its corruption [*alteration*]. And all the problems of pedagogy in *Emile* may

> be summarized in this fact. The child is at first passive, the example engraves itself within the memory, "*waiting*" to enter the heart. It may remain in the memory without entering the heart; and conversely, because of the resemblance between the heart and memory, the child may feign feeling from the heart when he actually contents himself with imitating according to the signs of memory. He may always content himself with *giving signs*.[49]

For Kant as well as Rousseau, while imitation is pedagogically necessary, it also harbors the seeds of a fundamental corruption of morality. Consequently, there is an attempt to distinguish between a good imitation and a bad one, an essential and natural mimesis and one that is the product of a moral corruption. But as Derrida has shown, mimesis is a structural condition of possibility for moral behavior at all; consequently, the attempt to determine this "bad mimesis" as a perversion and an accident amounts to a disavowal of the quasi-transcendental status of mimesis.[50]

Derrida's reading of Kant thus far has concerned not Kant's determination of the moral principle itself, but rather the difficulties involved in Kant's attempt to determine whether moral action ever takes place. Derrida reads Kant to the effect that there is no "example" of the moral law, no certitude of the actual occurrence of the categorical imperative, and no way to know whether any act is done out of duty or merely in conformity to duty. Of course, these are all one and the same problem. For Kant, this problem derives from the fact that, by linking morality to the principles upon which the will acts and not the actions themselves, the ability to determine whether an action is moral or not runs up against a phenomenal limit. To put it crudely, we can see actions, but not intentions; indeed, we cannot ever be apodictically certain of our own intentions. Derrida's contribution would be to understand this contaminability as not simply a function of the phenomenal limit, but a function of a structural necessity: there is no moral law, no moral action, without the possibility of imitation, deception, secret motives—in short, no morality without the possibility of immorality. Though this may be a conclusion that is already prepared, as it were, by Kant's text itself, it nevertheless remains that there is in Kant an attempt to reduce to a mere accident what nonetheless remains a structural necessity. This is apparent when Kant attempts to maintain a rigorous distinction between acting out of duty and acting in conformity with duty, thereby eliminating the corrupting effects of mimesis. And it will be true as well when Kant attempts to keep rational religion free from the corruption of dogmatic faith and material religion.

V

There is an additional difficulty that needs to be addressed. I noted earlier that Derrida associates the unconditional demand with the Kantian categorical imperative. And yet, while categorical imperatives are indeed, for Kant, unconditional, they nevertheless do not represent an infinite responsibility to the singularity of the other. Consequently, if there is a Levinasian coloring to Derrida's employment of the word "unconditional," then Derrida's association of the unconditional demand with the Kantian categorical imperative could only signify an egregious misunderstanding of Kantian ethics. This is because for Kant, far from commanding an infinite responsibility to a singular other, the categorical imperative commands respect for the law that is, by definition, general and universalizable; thus the first formulation of the categorical imperative reads: "*act only in accordance with that maxim through which you can at the same time will that it become a universal law.*"[51] And even though another formulation of the categorical imperative will command one to "*act that you use humanity, whether in your own person or in the person of any other, always at the same time as an end, never merely as a means,*"[52] this formulation defines responsibility to the other not in terms of the other's singularity, but in terms of the other's status as an end in himself, i.e., another autonomous and self-legislating being. It is thus what is precisely most universal among humanity that is the concern of the categorical imperative, not the singularity of the other. So how can Derrida claim a proximity to Kant here?

The answer is that the unconditional in Derrida's sense, while it is the *sine qua non* of any thinking of the ethical, never takes place as such independent of the law. The unconditional as a responsibility to the singularity of the other, then, is impossible. One cannot think the unconditional without universality and law, and, therefore, without a certain Kantianism. This is precisely the criticism that Derrida levels against Levinas. And yet, without the thought of this unconditional as infinite responsibility, the possibility of justice is foreclosed. Consequently, ethics involves thinking together the unconditionality of infinite responsibility and the need to calculate and mediate in a universal way with the competing claims of multiple others to whom one is responsible. This becomes abundantly clear in Derrida's "Force of Law."

"Force of Law" was originally a paper that Derrida delivered at the Cardozo Law School in 1989 for a colloquium on "Deconstruction and the Possibility of Justice." This text is especially notable for being the place in which Derrida most directly dispels certain confusions about, and criticisms of, deconstruction, particularly the charge that deconstruction is fundamentally destructive and nihilistic. For those inclined to such a reading of deconstruction, Derrida's claim in "Force of Law" that "*Deconstruction is justice*" will certainly come as a surprise. How is one to understand this claim? The answer lies in the fact that Derrida's deconstruction is not carried out for its own sake, but is rather motivated by the demand for justice: "For in the end, where would deconstruction find its force, its movement or its motivation if not in this always unsatisfied appeal, beyond the given determinations of what one names, in determined contexts, justice, the possibility of justice?"[53] To understand this argument, it is necessary to probe the concepts of justice and law more deeply.

As I have argued, Derrida's claim that "deconstruction is justice" seems to endow deconstruction with some kind of ethico-political content. Strictly speaking, deconstruction in fact prescribes no such ethical injunctions. And yet, a deconstructive reading may nevertheless be undertaken on account of such an injunction. Therefore, while Derrida is certainly at the risk of being misunderstood here, it is not the case that "deconstruction is justice," but rather that Derrida's deconstructive reading is motivated by a passion for justice. This point will be clarified as the notion of "justice" is elaborated in more detail.

For Derrida, justice is not identical to the law. By way of anticipation, Derrida writes: "I want to insist at once to reserve the possibility of a justice, indeed of a law [*loi*] that not only exceeds or contradicts law but also, perhaps, has no relation to law, or maintains such a strange relation to it that it may just as well demand law as exclude it."[54] Why is it that justice and law need to be distinguished? It is not, on the surface, clear that these are two different things. For example, we commonly speak of someone being "brought to justice," which means nothing other than being tried "before the law." There are two explanations for why Derrida wishes to distinguish law and justice.

The first reason is that justice, for Derrida, is synonymous with the unconditional, and as such, addresses the singularity of the other; but the law by definition involves generality. Derrida explicitly associates this understanding of justice with Levinas's discourse, or, more accurately, says that he would be "tempted" to make such an association:

> I would be tempted, up to a certain point, to bring the concept of justice—which I am here trying to distinguish from law—closer to Levinas's. I would do so just because of this infinity and because of the heteronomic relation to the other [*autrui*], to the face of the other that commands me, whose infinity I cannot thematize and whose hostage I am [. . .] Levinas speaks of an infinite right in what he calls "Jewish

> humanism," whose basis is not "the concept 'man'" but rather the other [*autrui*]: "the extent of the other's right" is "practically an infinite right." Here *équité* is not equality, calculated proportion, equitable distribution or distributive justice, but rather, absolute dissymmetry. And the Levinasian notion of justice would rather come closer to the Hebrew equivalent of what we would perhaps translate as holiness [*sainteté*].[55]

But what is perhaps more interesting than Derrida's evocation of Levinas, which is not an assimilation but only the expression of a "temptation," is his immediate disavowal of Levinas: "But since I would have other difficult questions about Levinas' difficult discourse, I cannot be content to borrow a conceptual trait without risking confusions or analogies. And so I will go no further in this direction."[56] Why Derrida makes this disavowal will soon be clear. The important point for now is that Derrida wishes to divorce justice from law because the singularity that is the decisive component of justice is effaced in the generality of the law.

The second reason for Derrida's insistence on maintaining the distinction between justice and law is because of the inextricable link between law and "force." Derrida notes that the English expression "to enforce the law" demonstrates this link between law and force, a connection that is lost in the French *appliquer la loi*. To establish this claim, Derrida draws upon Kant, who has demonstrated "with the greatest rigor" the fact that there is no law without force. "There is no law that does not imply *in itself, a priori, in the analytic structure of its concept,* the possibility of being 'enforced,' applied by force."[57] Derrida refers here to paragraph E of Kant's "Introduction to the Theory of Right" in *The Metaphysics of Morals*.

The Metaphysics of Morals comprises two main parts, which Kant originally published separately, the "Metaphysical First Principles of the Doctrine of Right" and the "Metaphysical First Principles of the Doctrine of Virtue." This basic division involves a distinction between those duties that can be given (and enforced) by external laws and those duties that cannot be given externally. Kant uses the terms ethics or morality with respect to the latter. For Kant, morality cannot be enforced, precisely because the morality of a given action lies not in the *conformity with duty* (*pflichtmässig*) of an action, which alone is visible, but in an action being done *out of duty* (*aus Pflicht*), which cannot be seen, and therefore cannot be enforced.

Right, then, implies enforceability. But just because there is a law that is enforced does not make that law "right." Kant here makes a distinction between *positive right* and *natural right*. The first is an empirical science of actually existing laws, while the second alone can "supply the immutable principles for any giving of positive law." And for Kant, this immutable principle for any giving of positive law is as follows: "Any action is *right* if it can coexist with everyone's freedom in accordance with a universal law, or if on its maxim the freedom of choice of each can coexist with everyone's freedom in accordance with a universal law." Consequently, when a given action cannot coexist with the freedom of everyone in accordance with a universal law, there is an authorization of force to coerce someone who infringes upon freedom in accordance with universal laws. This principle of coercion, Kant maintains, is not a separate element from obligation in accordance with universal laws, as if right were composed of these two separate elements. Rather, "one can locate the concept of right directly in the possibility of connecting universal reciprocal coercion with the freedom of everyone."[58] Therefore, law (right) and force (coercion) are not two separate things, but the very concept of law contains within it the idea of coercion in accordance with this law.

But if Derrida finds in Kant a rigorous demonstration of the fundamental link between law and force, he will differ from Kant profoundly on one major point. On Kant's reading, the force that is entailed by the very concept of law finds its ultimate justification in the "immutable" and rational principles that found such law. This does not mean that all laws as they actually exist (positive right) are just; but Kant would no doubt maintain, at least in principle, that *natural* right, which supplies the rational and universal principles upon which all positive law is (ideally) based, and which is fundamentally linked to the moral principle as determined in Kant's ethics, is itself just. Here Derrida and Kant would part company. Not only would Derrida reject the distinction between positive and natural right; he even claims that deconstructive thought is primarily aimed at nothing other than this distinction. He writes that "deconstructive questioning"

> starts, as has been the case, by destabilizing or complicating the opposition between *nomos* and *physis,* between *thesis* and *physis*—that is to say, the opposition between law [*loi*], convention, the institution on the one hand, and nature on the other, with all the oppositions that they condition. An example—and this is only an example—is that between positive law and natural law (*différance* is the displacement of this oppositional logic).[59]

While it may be fundamentally necessary to think about right in terms of maximizing freedom in accordance with universal laws—Derrida will never simply *oppose* freedom, and says later that "nothing seems to me less outdated than the classical emancipatory ideal"[60]—the real question (though Derrida does not pose it as such in "Force of Law") is what transpires in the movement from natural to positive right. Natural right never exists as such without its inscription as positive right. But this inscription opens the possibility of corruption, of interpretation, and, ultimately, of a transgression of the very principles of so-called "natural right." Consequently, far from guaranteeing the morality of the law, natural right never takes place without the possibility of a fundamental immorality of the law.

Of course, the other reason to be suspicious of a discourse based on supposedly "natural" right is precisely that it "naturalizes" and thereby justifies what might be fundamentally unjust.[61] In fact, Derrida will argue that the establishment of law and authority occurs by way of a type of performative utterance. He writes:

> The operation that amounts to founding, inaugurating, justifying law, to *making law*, would consist of a *coup de force*, of a performative and therefore interpretive violence that in itself is neither just nor unjust and that no justice and no earlier and previously founding law, no preexisting foundation, could, by definition, guarantee or contradict or invalidate. No justificatory discourse could or should ensure the role of metalanguage in relation to the performativity of institutive language or to its dominant interpretation.[62]

In other words, the moment at which law is instituted is a *founding* moment that is itself neither legal nor illegal. Perhaps the clearest example would be the founding of a new state or regime, or a declaration of independence:[63] independence, and the founding of the new state, depends upon the performative act that declares it as such. This founding moment may justify itself based upon earlier conventions, but these conventions are only themselves based upon similar moments of performative auto-foundation. And it is this performative force that Derrida refers to as "mystical," drawing from Montaigne's phrase, the "mystical foundation of authority." Montaigne writes: "Lawes are now maintained in credit, not because they are just, but because they are lawes. It is the mystical foundation of their authority; they have none other . . . Whosoever obeyeth them because they are just, obeyes them not justly the way he ought [sic]."[64]

Consequently, the origin of authority or the positing of law cannot by definition have anything as its foundation other than itself; authority is self-grounding, which is to say, it has no foundation. It is for this reason that Derrida says that the law is essentially *deconstructible*, both because law is founded on interpretable textual strata (the history of law), and, more fundamentally, because the ultimate foundation of law is by definition unfounded. Derrida underlines that the fact that the law is deconstructible is not a *bad* thing, since it is this deconstructibility that makes progress and change possible.[65] But it is not the deconstructibility of law alone that makes deconstruction possible; it is also, Derrida says, the undeconstructibility of justice. Justice is that in the name of which the deconstruction of the law takes place; consequently, deconstruction can be said to take place "in the interval that separates the undeconstructibility of justice from the deconstructibility of the law."[66] Derrida writes:

> [T]his "idea of justice" seems indestructible in its affirmative character, in its demand of gift without exchange, without circulation, without recognition or gratitude, without economic circularity, without calculation and without rules, without reason and without theoretical rationality, in the sense of regulating mastery. And so one can recognize in it, even accuse in it a madness, and perhaps another kind of mysticism [*un autre sorte de mystique*]. And deconstruction is mad about and from such justice, mad about and from this desire for justice.[67]

It is in the name of this infinite (because unconditional) responsibility to the other that deconstruction takes place. And because this justice is an infinite responsibility to the other, it is always directed towards singularity, "to the singularity of the other."[68]

In "Force of Law," Derrida distinguishes law and justice both because the singularity to which justice is addressed is betrayed in the generality of the law, and because of the link between law and force, the ever-present possibility that what takes place in the name of law is a violent oppression. Yet, while it is necessary to distinguish between law and justice, it is not, in fact, possible to draw such a rigorous demarcation: "Everything would still be simple if this distinction between justice and law were a true distinction, an opposition the functioning of which was logically regulated and masterable. But it turns out that law claims to exercise itself in the name of justice and that justice demands for itself that it be established in the name of a law that must be put to work [*mis en oeuvre*] (constituted and applied) by force 'enforced.'"[69]

But why is it that justice demands for itself that it be established in the name of a law that must be "enforced"? The first reason is that justice is essentially "weak." In the course of his analysis in "Force of Law," Derrida reflects on Pascal's *pensée* fragment 298, which reads:

> *Justice, force*—It is right that what is just should be followed; it is necessary that what is strongest should be followed. Justice without force is powerless; force without justice is tyrannical. Justice without force is gainsaid, because there are always offenders; force without justice is

> condemned. It is necessary then, to combine justice and force; and for this end make what is just strong, or what is strong just.[70]

Derrida attempts to "retrieve" this *pensée* from the conventional interpretation that sees in it "the sort of pessimistic, relativistic, and empiricist skepticism that drove Arnaud to suppress these pensées in the Port Royal edition, alleging that Pascal wrote them under the impression of a reading of Montaigne, according to whom laws [*lois*] are not in themselves just but are rather just only because they are laws." Just as Derrida appropriates Montaigne's argument for the performative foundation of authority, so too, in Pascal, Derrida finds "the premises of a *modern* critical philosophy, even a critique of juridical ideology, a desedimentation of the superstructures of law that both hide and reflect the economic and political interests of the dominant forces of society."[71]

The net result, however, of the dissociation of law and justice, the association of law and force, and the impotence of a justice without force, is that for justice to be possible, it must take place by way of a complicity with the law; otherwise, it risks never taking place at all. This is why Derrida says that deconstruction operates between two poles, that of the calculable (law) and that of the incalculable (justice), and that it is necessary to think these two together: "law is the element of calculation, and it is just that there be law, but justice is incalculable, it demands that one calculate with the incalculable." "Calculating with the incalculable," of course, is logically impossible, which is why Derrida calls justice "an experience of the impossible" and an "experience of aporia."[72]

It might seem that the type of decision that is paradigmatic for Derrida when he speaks of "calculating with the incalculable" is an extreme one that we might not encounter every day; but this is not the case. Every legal or ethical judgment involves deciding whether or not a singular case falls under a general rule. And not only is one forced to make a decision between the singularity of the case and the generality of the rule, but one actually performatively re-founds or re-creates the law in the application of it. Derrida writes:

> To be judged, the decision of a judge, for example, must not only follow a rule of law or a general law [*loi*] but must also assume it, approve it, confirm its value, by a reinstituting act of interpretation, as if, at the limit, the law [*loi*] did not exist previously—as if the judge invented it in each case. Each exercise of justice as law can be just only if it is a "fresh judgment" (I borrow this English expression from Stanley Fish's article, "Force"). This new freshness, the initiality of this inaugural judgment can very well—better yet, must [*doit*] very well—conform to a pre-

> existing law [*loi*], but the reinstituting, reinventive and freely deciding interpretation of the responsible judge requires that his "justice" not consist only in conformity, in the conservative and reproductive activity of judgment. In short, for a decision to be just and responsible, it must [*il faut*], in its proper moment, if there is one, be both regulated and without regulation, it must preserve the law [*loi*] and also destroy or suspend it enough to have [*pour devoir*] to reinvent it in each case, rejustify it, reinvent it at least in the reaffirmation and the new and free confirmation of its principle. Each case is other, each decision is different and requires an absolutely unique interpretation, which no existing, coded rule can or ought to guarantee absolutely. (At least, if the rule does guarantee it in a secure fashion, then the judge is a calculating machine.)[73]

This passage brings us back to the key issue in "Passions," namely, the fact that even being polite or friendly requires not simply that one conform to the rules of friendship or politeness, nor even that one act out of respect for those rules, but that one "invent without rule." It now becomes clear why Derrida makes this claim, and why it seems that conforming to or even acting out of respect for the rules of friendship is not sufficient: it fails to account for the singularity of the other that one addresses.

If the just decision involves not the mere application of a rule, but also a reinvention of the law in the face of the singularity of the case, then we can say that at no moment is one guaranteed that the decision made is just. This is not simply because the necessary complicity with the law fails to account completely for the singularity of the case, but also because, following Derrida's analysis of the performative autofoundation of the law, nothing can guarantee the justice of the law one has reinvented. Just as the founding moment in a new political regime is, as such, neither legal nor illegal, so too there is no "rule" to guarantee the justice of the rule that one "reinvents" by applying this rule to a particular case. There can be no guarantee of the justice of the decision, and no good conscience. Therefore Derrida speaks, following Kierkegaard, of the "madness of decision" and the "ordeal of the undecidable" that haunts every decision.[74] Derrida writes:

> At no moment, it seems, can a decision be said to be present and fully just: either it has not yet been made according to a rule, and nothing allows one to call it just, or it has already followed a rule—whether given, received, confirmed, preserved, or reinvented—which, in its turn, nothing guarantees absolutely; and, moreover, if it were guaranteed, the decision would have turned back into calculation and one could not call it just. That is why the test and ordeal of the undecidable, of which I have

> just said that it must be gone through by any decision worthy of this name, is never past or passed [*passée ou dépassée*], it is not a surmounted or sublated [*relevé*] (*aufgehoben*) moment in the decision. The undecidable remains caught, lodged, as a ghost at least, but an essential ghost, in every decision, in every event of decision.[75]

VI

In "Passions," in addition to the sustained interrogation of the question of duty in Kant, Derrida also offers some more general remarks on the question of "deconstruction and ethics":

> One can today, in many different places, attend to or participate in a congenial and disturbing task: restoring morality and, especially, reassuring those who had serious reasons for being troubled by this topic. Some souls believe themselves to have found in Deconstruction ["*la*" *Déconstruction*]—as if there were one, and only one—a modern form of immorality, of amorality, or of irresponsibility (etc.: a discourse too well known; I do not need to continue), while others, more serious, in less of a hurry, better disposed toward so-called Deconstruction, today claim the opposite; they discern encouraging signs and in increasing numbers (at times, I must admit, in some of my texts) which would testify to a permanent, extreme, direct, or oblique, in any event, increasingly intense attention, to those things which one could identify under the fine names of "ethics," "morality," "responsibility," "subject," etc.[76]

There is no doubt that in "Force of Law," for example, Derrida tries to articulate an understanding of deconstruction that links it fundamentally to an affirmation of justice. This is a challenge to those who would see deconstruction as an amoral or immoral enterprise. But is "Force of Law" then to be taken as offering a type of "deconstructive morality"? Can one say that deconstruction is fundamentally concerned with articulating an ethics?

In this chapter, I have argued above all that Derrida's intervention in questions of ethics, and particularly in the Kantian determination of the concept of duty, has led to the destabilization of any form of "good conscience." Not only is one never sure of having acted morally (and this for structural and not simply empirical reasons), so too can one never be sure of the justice of any particular decision. This too is not accidental but inheres in the heterogeneity of law and justice. But if law and justice are heterogeneous, and yet the ethical decision involves making a decision that holds together law and justice, one can never be sure of having acted justly. Duty and responsibility, then, can never be simply discharged; rather, responsibility always remains haunted by undecidability.

It is for this reason that deconstruction cannot articulate an "ethics," at least if ethics is taken to mean the determination of duties that a rational and autonomous subject is capable of performing. The ethical demand, according to Derrida, is impossible because it involves calculating with the incalculable. This impossibility does not free one from responsibility; but it does prevent the ethical "subject" from ever taking full measure of his responsibility and strictly delimiting his duties. And it is for this reason that there is perhaps no such thing as an ethical "subject," if by this we understand a rational and autonomous being capable of both determining and executing his duty according to a set of definable criteria.

This does not prevent deconstruction, however, from having any ethical import; but this is very different from constituting an ethics. While Derrida will not deny that deconstruction has ramifications for ethics and responsibility, he will resist any association of deconstruction to a moralizing discourse:

> [I]t would be necessary to declare in the most direct way that if one had the *sense* of duty, and of responsibility, it would compel breaking with both these moralisms, with these two restorations of morality, including, therefore, the remoralization of deconstruction, which naturally seems more attractive than that to which it is rightly opposed, but which at each moment risks reassuring itself in order to reassure the other and to promote the consensus of a new dogmatic slumber. And it is so that one not be in too much of a hurry to say that it is in the name of a *higher* responsibility and a more intractable [*intraitable*] moral exigency that one declares one's distaste, uneven as it may be, for both moralisms.[77]

It is in the name of a "sense" of duty, then, that Derrida would break with two "moralisms": the moralism that denounces deconstruction as immoral, and the moralism that finds a fundamental morality in deconstruction. Derrida's priority is to avoid any self-assurance in the matter of one's responsibility to the other, and to keep in play the undecidability and incalculability of every ethical demand. If ethics involves the determination and delimitation of duties, if the philosophical gesture involves a circumscription of the ethical, then Derrida's thinking attempts to keep the question of ethics and responsibility *open:*

> All this, therefore, still remains open, suspended, undecided, questionable, even beyond the question, indeed [. . .] absolutely aporetic. What is the ethicity of ethics? The morality of morality? What is responsibility? What is the "What is" in this case? etc. These questions are always urgent. In a certain way they must remain urgent and unanswered, at any rate without a general and rule-governed response, without a response other than that which is linked specifically each time, to the occurrence of a decision without rules and without will in the course of a new test of the undecidable. And let it not be said too precipitately that these questions or these propositions are *already* inspired by a concern that could by right be called ethical, moral, responsible, etc. For sure, in saying that ("And let it not be said too precipitately . . . " etc.), one gives ammunition to the officials of anti-deconstruction, but all in all isn't that preferable to the constitution of a consensual euphoria or, worse, a community of complacent deconstructionists, reassured and reconciled with the world in ethical certainty, good conscience, satisfaction of service rendered, and the consciousness of duty accomplished (or, more heroically still, yet to be accomplished)?[78]

While for Derrida ethics is impossible, caught in the aporia between justice and law, this impossibility does not obviate the need for decision there where there can be no guarantee that one's decision is the right one. If there is a difference that should be underlined between Kant and Derrida, it is this: whereas Kant's ethical thinking operates on the basis of the principle "ought implies can," which is to say, we know that ethical action is *possible* because the moral law obligates us, for Derrida, we remain responsible despite the impossibility of justice. In other words, what commands us unconditionally, the injunction that, for Derrida, prescribes deconstructing, is unconditional despite this very impossibility.

4

Faith, Messianicity, and Radical Evil: The "Kantian" Transposition

I

In "Faith and Knowledge," Derrida inquires into the very sources of the religious, in an attempt to uncover the fundamental structure of "religiosity." And yet he proceeds with a sense of caution or "restraint" that is made a theme within text itself. Derrida begins "Faith and Knowledge" by asking: "*How 'to talk religion'? Of religion? Singularly of religion, today? How dare we speak of it in the singular without fear and trembling, this very day? And so briefly and so quickly? Who would be so imprudent as to claim that the issue here is both identifiable and new? Who would be so presumptuous as to rely on a few aphorisms?*"[1] Similarly, he begins the second part by directly invoking the need for a certain reticence or scruple with regard to this concept.

> **Religion?** Here and now, this very day, if one were still supposed to *speak* of it, of religion, perhaps one could attempt to think it in *itself* or to devote oneself to this task. No doubt, but to try above all to *say* it and to *utter a verdict* concerning it, with the necessary rigor, which is to say, with the reticence, modesty, respect or fervour, in a word the scruple (*religio*) demanded at the very least by that which is or claims to be, in its essence, a religion. As its name indicates, it would be necessary, therefore, one would be tempted to conclude, to speak of this essence with a sort of *religio*-sity. In order not to introduce anything alien, leaving it thus intact, safe, *unscathed*.[2]

In light of this reticence, it comes as something of a surprise when, shortly thereafter, Derrida writes:

> Religion, in the *singular*? Response: 'Religion is **the response**.' Is it not there, perhaps, that we must seek the beginning of a response? Assuming, that is, that we know what *responding* means, and also *responsibility*. Assuming, that is, that one knows it—and believes in it. No response, indeed, without a principle of responsibility: one must respond to the

> other, before the other and for oneself. And no responsibility without a *given word,* a sworn faith, <*foi jurée*>, without a pledge, without an oath, without some *sacrament* or *ius iurandum.*[3]

This passage is crucial for an understanding of "Faith and Knowledge." Despite all of the hesitations, Derrida ultimately responds to the question of the meaning of religion by linking it to responsibility. But the definition of religion as response is itself a response: "Response: 'Religion is **the response.**'"

If religion is linked to the response and therefore responsibility, then one can already anticipate that such religion will be caught in the same quasi-transcendental aporia as justice. On the one hand, responsibility addresses the other in his singularity; and yet, the responsibility to any singular other involves a sacrifice of other others. This sacrifice of other others means that one is forced to calculate with a responsibility that must nevertheless remain incalculable. Responsibility—and by extension, religion—is therefore, like justice, impossible. Concerning this relationship between responsibility and sacrifice, Derrida writes, in *The Gift of Death:*

> [W]hat binds me thus in my singularity to the absolute singularity of the other, immediately propels me into the space or risk of absolute sacrifice. There are also others, an infinite number of them, the innumerable generality of others to whom I should be bound by the same responsibility, a general and universal responsibility (what Kierkegaard calls the ethical order). I cannot respond to the call, the request, the obligation, or even the love of another without sacrificing the other other, the other others.[4]

While for Kant the notion of religion derives from the moral law, Derrida's understanding of religion derives from the notion of the unconditional and its aporetic relationship to the generality of the law.

Derrida posits two sources of "religion." These two sources are not faith and knowledge, as the title misleadingly suggests, but faith (or belief) and holiness (or sacredness). Derrida writes that "religion" marks the "convergence of two experiences that are generally equally held to be equally religious": "the experience of *belief,* on the one hand (believing or credit, the fiduciary or the trustworthy in the act of faith, fidelity, the appeal to blind confidence, the testimonial that is always beyond proof, demonstrative reason, intuition)"; and "the experience of the unscathed, of *sacredness* or of *holiness,* on the other." These two sources ultimately correspond to two etymological derivations of the word "religion." "Faith," on the one hand, relates to the derivation of *religio* from *religare*, "linking religion to the *link*, precisely, to obligation, ligament, and hence to obligation, to debt, etc., between men or between man and God"; holiness, on the other hand, relates to the Ciceronian derivation of *religio* from *relegere*, "bringing together in order to return and begin again; whence *religio*, scrupulous attention, respect, patience, even modesty, shame or pity." "Religion," therefore, figures as the ellipse of these two sources "because it both comprehends the two foci but also sometimes shrouds their irreducible duality in silence."[5]

II

Derrida's concern in "Faith and Knowledge" is with a type of originary faith, and in particular, with the presence of this originary faith in every encounter with the other. If "religion is the response," then it is the case that religion is linked necessarily to faith: "No response, indeed, without a principle of responsibility: one must respond to the other, before the other and for oneself. And no responsibility without a *given word*, a sworn faith <*foi jurée*>, without a pledge, without an oath, without some *sacrament* or *ius iurandum*."[6] Derrida will ultimately demonstrate that there is a type of "I promise the truth" implied in every address to the other.

The language of performativity is essential to Derrida's concept of faith. The distinction between "performative" and "constative" utterances derives from the work of John Austin, whose Harvard lectures, posthumously published as *How to Do Things with Words*, was the object of Derrida's analysis in "Signature Event Context." The performative utterance is an utterance that does not describe, report, or constate anything (and hence can be neither true nor false), but rather is, or is part of, the doing of an action.[7] The clearest examples of such performative utterances are those tied to a particular ceremony or ritual, such as a wedding or the naming of a ship, where the ritual is not accomplished until the appropriate words are uttered. Thus, "I do" in a wedding ceremony, according to Austin's analysis, does not describe a state of affairs; rather, the very uttering of the words performs the action.

In spite of the somewhat critical tone of "Signature Event Context," Derrida invokes the performative in many of his texts, putting the notion to positive use while at the same time pointing to its limitations. And the target of Derrida's criticism in "Signature Event Context" is not the notion of the performative as such, but rather Austin's exclusion of so-called "parasitic" uses of the performative. Austin writes:

> As *utterances* our performatives are *also* heir to certain other kinds of ill which infect *all* utterances. And these likewise, though again they might be brought into a more general account, we are deliberately at present excluding. I mean, for example, the following: a performative utterance will, for example, be *in a peculiar way* hollow or void if said by an actor on the stage, or if introduced in a poem, or spoken in soliloquy. [. . .] Language in such circumstances is in special ways—intelligibly—used not seriously, but in ways *parasitic* upon its normal use—ways which fall under the doctrines of the *etiolations* of language. All this we are *excluding* from consideration.[8]

These parasitic usages amount to a repetition of the performative utterance outside of the context of conditions necessary for it to be successful or "felicitous" as a performative utterance. For example, when two people are married in a movie, the actors are not thereby married in real life. It becomes necessary, then, to specify the conditions under which a performative utterance is successful.

Austin provides six conditions necessary for the success of a performative utterance, some of which are necessary for the actual performative to take place at all, including an accepted conventional procedure, the presence of participants qualified to undertake the procedure, and the complete carrying out of the procedure. Without these, the performance cannot be said to have taken place, as, for example, when a woman who says "I do" during the marriage ceremony is already married to another person. Austin refers to the result of a failure to meet these conditions as a "misfire" of the performative utterance. However, there are other conditions which, when not satisfied, do not annul the result of the performative utterance, but constitute an "abuse" of the performative. This occurs in cases where a certain intention is required on the part of the speaker and/or in cases where the performative commits one to certain future actions. For example, if someone says "I bet you twenty dollars" but has no intention of paying up should he lose the bet, then, while this counts as an "abuse" of the procedure, the bet is nevertheless binding, and the performance was therefore a successful one.[9]

Derrida's objection to Austin's analysis in "Signature Event Context" does not amount to a rejection of the performative as such, but rather an objection to the idea that one can make a rigorous distinction between normal and parasitic uses of the performative. A parasitic use of the performative consists in the repetition of the utterance outside of its proper context. Derrida argues, however, that since it is a condition of possibility of language as such that it is capable of repetition and, therefore, repetition outside of all "context," then it becomes *a priori* impossible to rigorously distinguish between normal and parasitic uses. "For, finally, is not what Austin excludes as anomalous, exceptional, 'non-serious,' that is, *citation* (on the stage, in a poem, or in a soliloquy), the determined modification of a general citationality—or rather, a general iterability—without which there would not even be a 'successful' performative?" For Derrida, the performative utterance would not be possible if the utterance could not be recognized as conforming to a model and a convention; therefore, the possibility for the utterance to be cited and repeated is the *conditio sine qua non* of the performative utterance. This does not mean that there is not a "relative purity" of performatives, but rather that one cannot simply oppose citation or iteration to the noniteration, the pure presence, of the performative event.[10] This is of course structurally identical to Derrida's comments regarding the *aus Pflicht/pflichtmässig* distinction in Kant; if the morality of an act is only determined by the intention to act out of respect for the moral law, and moral action is only possible if there is at least an *a priori possibility* that the agent can act otherwise, then there is always the threat that the supposedly pure moral action may become a mere simulacrum of moral action, mere "conformity to duty." The possibility of the simulacrum is constitutive of the performative utterance just as it is of moral action, and, therefore, one can no more isolate a "pure performative" than one can isolate a "pure moral action." This deconstructive reading of Austin constitutes a first stage of Derrida's engagement with speech act theory; the second stage, essential to the present discussion of "faith," is Derrida's attempt to show that the so-called constative utterance is itself in a crucial sense already performative.

"Promising" belongs to a class of performative utterances that Austin calls "commissives" precisely because they commit one to some future action.[11] Promises, unlike constative statements, cannot properly be said to be true or false. And there are conditions that must obtain for a promise to be successful as a performative; for example, it is not possible, in most cases, for someone to promise in another's place. The same holds true for giving testimony, which is related to the promise: it is not possible to give testimony in a court of law in place of someone else. Testimony requires the presence of the witness himself.

What Derrida tries to demonstrate, in "Faith and Knowledge" and in other texts, is that every constative statement carries with it a promise. Consequently, every engagement with the other also involves a corresponding act of faith in the testimony of the other:

> The act of faith demanded in bearing witness exceeds, through its structure, all intuition and all proof, all knowledge ('I swear that I am telling

> the truth, not necessarily the "objective truth", but the truth of what I believe to be the true, I am telling you this truth, believe me, believe what I believe, there, where you will never be able to see nor know the irreplaceable yet universalizable, exemplary place from which I speak to you; perhaps my testimony is false, but I am sincere and in good faith, it is not false <as> testimony'). What therefore does the promise of this axiomatic (quasi-transcendental) performative do that conditions and foreshadows 'sincere' declarations no less than lies and perjuries, and thus all address of the other? It amounts to saying: 'Believe what I say as one believes in a miracle.'[12]

Derrida's argument here has something in common with the pragmatic analysis of language in analytic philosophy, and in particular with the theory of implicature, insofar as he is concerned with what is implied in any utterance, even if it is not explicitly contained in the utterance as such. Although Derrida does not mention it, a good example of this is found in Austin, where he notes that the statement "The cat is on the mat" implies that the person uttering the statement believes that the cat is on the mat. One cannot say, "The cat is on the mat but I do not believe it is."[13] This is referred to as implication rather than entailment, because in the case of logical entailment, if *p* entails *q*, then *~q* entails *~p*. On the other hand, if one says, "The cat is on the mat but I do not believe it is," not believing the cat is on the mat does not necessarily mean that the cat is not on the mat. Implication, therefore, operates in a different way than entailment.

Austin's example is significant precisely because it concerns "belief." The constative utterance implies that one believes what one is saying, and in this way, when addressed to another (or even to oneself as other), is a type of promise or testimony. Regardless of whether or not the cat is on the mat, an address to the other that says "the cat is on the mat" implies that the speaker believes this to be the truth, whether or not it is in fact the truth, and therefore asks the addressee in his turn to believe in the veracity (the "*meaning to say* the truth," as opposed to "the truth") of the statement: "Believe what I say as one believes in a miracle."

It is possible in this way to inscribe Derrida within a tradition of pragmatic analysis in the style of Austin and Grice,[14] a gesture made even more plausible by his concern with indexicality in his early work, especially *Speech and Phenomena.*[15] It should be said, however, that for Derrida, it is not simply the case that "I believe that the cat is on the mat" is implied in the statement "the cat is on the mat," especially if the implied meaning is understood as an *additional* meaning grafted onto the basic denotation of the utterance. Rather, belief is the transcendental condition of any communication whatsoever, and, therefore, of any basic constative meaning. In other words, communication would not be possible at all if one could not have faith in the veracity of the other's statements. Therefore, the performative or testimonial character of the address to the other is not added on to the constative statement, but is the condition of possibility of the constative statement as such. Derrida writes: "Without the performative experience of this elementary act of faith, there would neither be 'social bond' nor address of the other, nor any performativity in general: neither convention, nor institution, nor constitution, nor sovereign state, nor law."[16] For Austin, the performative relies upon socially determined conventions and norms; but the performativity that Derrida speaks of here is a performativity that must "precede" the performatives that Austin analyzes, since conventions could not be established without this transcendental performativity that is the condition of all communication.

This transcendental performativity is, in fact, only quasi-transcendental, since it is not only the condition of possibility of communication but also its condition of impossibility. This does not mean that communication does not happen, but rather that there is no "pure communication" without the possibility of interruption, dissemination, and loss of meaning. In this sense, Derrida's deconstructive reading of Austin in "Signature Event Context" applies to Derrida's own notion of performativity as much as it does to Austin's. In other words, if any address to the other presupposes a testimonial performativity and an act of faith, it nevertheless remains the case that one can *lie* to the other. There is nothing to preclude this possibility, not simply because humans are capable of dissimulation, but because performativity as such requires iterability and therefore the possibility of repetition.

The originary performativity of the promise therefore relies upon what Derrida calls elsewhere—with reference to another term for this originary performativity, namely, the "yes"—the "gramophone effect." In "Ulysses Gramophone," Derrida underscores the repetition necessary for any promise to function. He writes of the "yes":

> It must *a priori* and immediately confirm its promise and promise its confirmation. This essential repetition lets itself be haunted by an intrinsic threat, by an internal telephone which parasites it like its mimetic, mechanical double, like its incessant parody. We shall return to this fatality. But we can already hear a gramophony which records writing in the liveliest voice. *A priori* it reproduces it, in the absence of intentional presence on the part of the affirmer. Such gramophony responds, of course, to the dream of a reproduction which *preserves* as

> its truth the living *yes,* archived in the very quick of its voice. But by the same token it allows the possibility of parody, of a *yes* technique that persecutes the most spontaneous, the most giving desire of the *yes*. To meet [*répondre à*] its destination, this *yes* must reaffirm itself immediately. Such is the condition of a signed commitment. The *yes* can only state *itself* by promising itself its own memory. The affirmation of the *yes* is the affirmation of memory. *Yes* must preserve itself, and thus reiterate itself, archive its voice in order to allow it once again to be heard. This is what I call the gramophone effect. *Yes* gramophones itself and telegramophones itself, *a priori.*[17]

The promise only functions as a promise if it can be archived (recorded, "gramophoned") and then repeated at a later point as a confirmation of the promise, or as a countersignature. Iterability is therefore a necessary condition for any promise as such. The promise must be repeatable. But the necessary repeatability of the promise means that there is always the possibility of promises being made that, to adopt Austin's language, represent an "abuse" of this performativity. False promises and counterfeit signatures are the always possible result of a communication that works only on the basis of an *a priori* iterability.

III

The performative nature of the address to the other clarifies Derrida's use of the Kantian phrase "radical evil." In "Faith and Knowledge," Derrida does not provide any extended analysis of the question of radical evil, and does not set out to defend or refute Kant's thesis. But there is, in the scattered remarks he makes throughout the text, a significant transposition of this key concept of Kant's *Religion.* Noting that Kant's *Religion* was, in addition to a treatise on religion, also a book on radical evil, Derrida asks, in a parenthetical remark, "What of reason and of radical evil today? And [what] if the 'return of the religious' was not without relation to the return—modern or postmodern, for once—of certain phenomena, at least, of radical evil? Does radical evil destroy or institute the possibility of religion?" This final question is left hanging here, unanswered. But a few pages later, Derrida makes reference to the "*possibility* of that **radical evil** without which nothing good could be done [trans. modified]."[18]

Peter Fenves rightly notes that Derrida stresses *possibility* here; what is at stake in Derrida's text is not the "facticity" of radical evil, a facticity that Kant tried unsuccessfully to prove, but a possibility of radical evil which, rather than simply undermining the good, is the condition of doing good at all.[19] How are we to make sense of this? The answer lies in the foregoing analysis of Derrida's notion of faith. Derrida defines faith in terms of the promise to tell the truth—and the corresponding credit or belief in this promise—that is presupposed for any address to the other to take place at all. But since the performativity of the promise only functions on the condition of iterability and repetition—which make it a priori *possible* that this performative is being abused, i.e., that one is promising without intending to keep the promise—then the very condition of communication is the possibility of the lie.

For Kant, evil is linked not simply to failing to act in conformity with the law, but, perhaps even more perniciously in Kant's estimation, to dissimulating one's evil by acting in conformity with the law but not out of respect for the law. I have demonstrated the fundamental similarity between the *aus Pflicht/pflichmässig* distinction and the distinction between the successful performative and an "abuse" of the performative. In both cases, what is at stake is whether the intention behind the action was pure (in Kant's case, action out of respect for the law; in Austin's case, the use of a performative utterance, such as a promise, with the intention to carry out what is promised). Just as the possibility of the lie is the very condition of possibility of any truth-saying, of any veracity and therefore of any possible communication with the other, so too is any moral action at least predicated on the possibility that any lawful (general and repeatable) action is performed without the correct intention or motivation, without respect for the law. Therefore, according to Derrida, the exposure to the *possibility* of evil is a precondition for any relation to the other, and therefore of any moral action or responsibility. And because this evil must be possible in every instance without exception, this always-possible evil can be called "radical evil."

In the closing pages of "Faith and Knowledge," Derrida returns to the unanswered question, whether radical evil destroys or institutes the possibility of religion, concluding, as one might by now expect, that "the possibility of **radical evil** both destroys and institutes the religious."[20] If one understands the "religious," as Derrida does in "Faith and Knowledge," in terms of the relation to the other, then it is clear why the possibility of radical evil would both institute the religious and at the same time threaten this relation to the other and every social bond. The social bond, Derrida insists, is threatened by the very thing that makes it possible. In attacking the very thing that makes responsibility, veracity, and the social bond possible in the first place, Kant's attempt to foreclose the possibility of the lie furnishes an example of what Derrida calls "autoimmunization": the process whereby a living organism seeks to destroy that which sustains it.

IV

Kant's extreme opposition to the lie is readily evidenced in his notorious text from 1797, "On a Supposed Right to Lie from Philanthropy." In this text, Kant responds to a pamphlet written by the French politician and author Benjamin Constant, in which Constant argues that if the duty to tell the truth were taken unconditionally, society would be impossible. He finds proof for this proposition in "the very direct consequences drawn from this principle by a German philosopher, who goes so far as to maintain that it would be a crime to lie to a murderer who asked us whether a friend of ours whom he is pursuing has taken refuge in our house." The conclusion that Constant draws from the absurdity of such an idea is that "*To tell the truth is a duty, but only to one who has a right to the truth.*"[21] Oddly enough, while Constant's translator K. F. Kramer says in a footnote that Constant told him that the German philosopher referred to was Kant, and even though Kant himself claims to have said such a thing—"I hereby grant that I actually said this somewhere or other, though I cannot now recall where"[22]—no such argument can be found anywhere in Kant's writings.[23] Kant, taking responsibility for an argument he never made in the first place, famously sets out to defend the thesis that one cannot lie even to save a friend from a murderer who is pursuing him.

Derrida, who wrote extensively on the question of hospitality, was interested in this text precisely because it concerns a scene of hospitality: someone is given refuge in the home of a friend, and the question is whether there is an obligation to protect this guest from harm even if this should mean acting counter to what the moral law commands. What interests Derrida more specifically, however, is the precise reason why Kant argues for the unconditional prohibition of lying: to maintain the integrity of the social bond. Kant writes:

> Truthfulness in statements that one cannot avoid is a human being's duty to everyone, however great the disadvantage to him or to another that may result from it; and although I indeed do no wrong to him who unjustly compels me to make the statement if I falsify it, I nevertheless do wrong in the most essential part of duty *in general* by such falsification, which can therefore be called a lie (though not in a jurist's sense);

> that is, I bring it about, as far as I can, that statements (declarations) in general are not believed, and so too that all rights which are based on contracts come to nothing and lose their force; and this is a wrong inflicted upon humanity generally.[24]

It is interesting that Kant does not answer this question in terms of ethics, but in terms of right. While lying, from the perspective of ethics, is a violation of a duty to oneself, Kant is here concerned with a harm that is brought upon the other through the lie. But this "other" thereby harmed is not a specific person—indeed, Kant is willing to sacrifice a specific person, the friend in danger of being killed—but humanity in general. If one could not believe in the veracity of the other, no statement or declaration, and therefore no address to the other, could be believed, and consequently all rights and contracts upon which society is based would "come to nothing and lose their force." In short, the concession of even one permissible lie, any breach of the unconditional duty to tell the truth, threatens to unravel the social bond and eradicate the very basis of society.

In *Of Hospitality*, Derrida writes—precisely in line with his notion of "faith"—that this unconditional imperative to veracity, "even before being due to some normative prescription (which it is as well, of course), could be shown to be deduced from a simple, very simple *analysis* of speech, of a rhetorical, constative, descriptive address to the other, of its normativity or its intrinsic performativity." This is precisely the argument that Kant is making, according to Derrida: "Kant founds pure subjective morality, the duty to speak the truth to the other as an absolute duty of respect for the other and respect for the social bond; [. . .] he reminds us of its basis through an inflexible analysis of the structure of the speech act." And yet, handing over one's friend to his murderer remains something of a scandal for reason. This scandal, for Derrida, demonstrates precisely the aporia between law and justice. The unconditional demand to protect the other is, in Kant's thought, eradicated in the face of the universality of the law. In keeping with the "scene of hospitality" in this Kantian text, Derrida writes: "From the point of view of the law, the guest, even when he is well received, is first of all a foreigner, he must remain a foreigner. Hospitality is due to the foreigner, certainly, but remains, like the law, conditional, and thus conditioned in its dependence on the unconditionality that is the basis of the law."[25] Kant thus sacrifices the individual to the law, which is sacred and inviolable: "To be *truthful* (honest) in all declarations is therefore a sacred command of reason prescribing unconditionally, one not to be restricted by any conveniences."[26]

V

Kant's sacrifice in the name of the sacredness of the law leads to the concept of the holy, the second of Derrida's two sources of "religion." Derrida does not give a *single* definition of the holy, but rather variously employs the full range of meanings of the German *heilig:* holy, sacred, unscathed, immune, safe and sound, intact, indemnified, vital, fecund, fertile, and strong. Derrida does not suggest that the experience of the holy is necessarily "religious," nor does the experience of the holy necessarily entail an act of faith: "In principle, it is possible to sanctify, to sacralize the unscathed or to maintain oneself in the *presence* of the sacrosanct in various ways without bringing into play an act of belief, if at least belief, faith or fidelity signifies here acquiescing to the testimony of the other."[27]

Derrida associates the holy with the etymological derivation of *religio* from *relegere* as a returning or bringing together, as opposed to the derivation of *religio* from *religare* as a linking or joining, with which he associates faith. But Derrida notes that, whatever one decides concerning the etymology of *religio,* these

> competing etymologies can both be retraced to the same, and in a certain manner to the possibility of repetition, which produces the same as much as it confirms it. In both cases (*re-legere* and *re-ligare*), what is at issue is indeed a persistent bond that bonds itself first and foremost to itself. What is at issue is indeed a reunion <*rassemblement*>, a re-assembling, a re-collecting. A resistance or a reaction to disjunction. To ab-solute alterity.[28]

Both of these sources, then, represent a reaction to a prior disjunction, a disjunction that should be understood as the infinite alterity that separates one finite being from another. It is only because humans are originally disjoined that the movement toward the other and the establishment of the social bond requires the act of credit or faith examined above. So, too, holiness implies a separation, a restraint or a holding-back before that which must remain intact and indemnified. Derrida refers to this restraint before the holy as a "sacro-sanctifying attitude or intentionality," and this intentional attitude bears several names: "respect, modesty, restraint, inhibition, *Achtung* (Kant), *Scheu, Verhaltenheit, Gelassenheit* (Heidegger), restraint or *holding-back* <*halte*> in general."[29] Kant, for his part, repeatedly refers to the moral law as sacred, holy, and inviolable, and it is the holiness of the law that commands respect for the law.

Like faith, the holy as Derrida articulates it is not in itself identical to the holy in a religious sense, since it has no essential connection to God or the divine. Rather, in keeping with his response that "religion is the response," Derrida is concerned with the holy as the indemnification of the alterity of the other, particularly in the form of the injunction "Thou shalt not kill." The essential point to be grasped here is that both faith and the holy are not in themselves religious, but are rather, for Derrida, "structures of religiosity" that are the transcendental conditions of determinate religion. Concerning the "intentional attitudes" of restraint, inhibition, respect, etc., before the holy, Derrida writes: "For if they are not in themselves properly religious, they always open the possibility of the religious without ever being able to limit or restrain it."[30] Later, Derrida comments that these two sources render

> possible, but not necessary, something like a religion, which is to say, an instituted apparatus consisting of dogmas or of articles of faith that are both determinate and inseparable from a given historical *socius* (Church, clergy, socially legitimated authority, people, shared idiom, community of the faithful committed to the same faith and sanctioning the same history).[31]

In other words, insofar as the originary promise/faith structure, as well as a certain restraint before the other—at least in the form of the "thou shalt not kill"—are the preconditions of any community whatsoever, they make possible any determined, historical socius and therefore any religion. And yet, as transcendental conditions of possibility of any socius, they precede any particular division into religious/non-religious or sacred/profane.

Derrida continues that the holy is essentially related to "life," not simply the life of the individual, but more importantly, the life of the community. "The religion of the living—is this not a tautology?" Derrida writes that "One could, without being arbitrary, read, select, connect everything in the semantic genealogy of the unscathed—'saintly, sacred, safe and sound, *heilig, holy*'—that speaks of force, **life**-force, fertility, growth, augmentation, and above all *swelling,* in the spontaneity of erection or of pregnancy." Therefore the holy is essentially related to the injunction "thou shalt not kill," and even to "the 'fundamentalist' prohibition of abortion, of artificial insemination, of performative intervention in the genetic potential, even to the ends of gene therapy etc."[32]

And yet, in spite of the absolute respect for life, one nevertheless must take into account, "without even speaking of wars of religion, of their terrorisms and their killings," the "no less universal sacrificial vocation." How do we account for this absolute respect for life in the face of sacrifice and religious violence? The principle that accounts for this double movement (respect for life and sacrifice of life), Derrida says, is that "life has absolute value only if it is worth *more than* life." Human life only has value insofar as it breaks the plane of human life: "[Life] is sacred, holy, infinitely respectable only in the name of what is more than it and what is not restricted to the naturalness of the bio-zoological (sacrificeable) [. . .] Thus, respect of life in the discourses of religion as such concerns 'human life' only in so far as it bears witness, in some manner, to the infinite transcendence of that which is worth more than it (divinity, the sacrosanctness of the law)."[33]

This logic of sacrifice, wherein life can be sacrificed in the name of what is worth more than life, is clearly at work, according to Derrida, in Kant's ethics:

> **Violence** of sacrifice in the name of non-violence. Absolute respect enjoins first and foremost sacrifice of self, of one's most precious interest. If Kant speaks of the 'holiness' of the moral law, it is while explicitly holding a discourse on 'sacrifice', which is to say, on another instantiation of religion 'within the limits of reason *alone*': the Christian religion as the only 'moral' religion.[34]

Kant, therefore, even in his attempt to define religion within the limits of reason alone, nevertheless remains within the sacrificial logic common to evil "cultic" and "statutory" religion: humanity has value not on account of its bare, zoological life, but because it partakes of that which transcends life: the holy moral law. Those pathological desires and inclinations that pertain to the human in his specificity must be subordinated or sacrificed to the generality of the moral law. It is precisely this logic of sacrifice that justifies, for Kant, placing the sacredness of the duty to veracity above the individual life that might thereby be sacrificed. But this sacrifice of the individual in the name of the law is, as we have seen, also a sacrifice of the individual in the name of the integrity of the social bond.

For Derrida, the very notion of community, like that of democracy, involves a notion of commonality, but at the same time remains composed of irreducible singularities. Thus the very idea of a community is aporetic. The social bond is founded on a prior disjunction, the mutual alterity of these singularities. And if the community is made possible on the basis of a certain performative promise that in its turn requires an act of credit or belief, it nevertheless remains that this alterity is never simply absorbed in the community, and that, as a condition of possibility of this social bond, there is the potential for a radical evil that threatens the community. Nevertheless, Derrida still makes use of the "impossible" idea of a universalizable culture of singularities, which is the object of a certain messianic expectation that remains irreducible to any actual, determinate messianism.

VI

The messianic, or "messianicity," is a term that figures frequently in Derrida's writings from 1993 on. The concept presents some interpretive difficulties, since it is a religious term that nevertheless designates a structure of experience that supposedly remains heterogeneous to any religious discourse; moreover, the basic idea that this term designates was already present in Derrida's earlier writings, though the word "messianic" itself does not appear. What, then, is Derrida doing in employing this word?[35]

Caputo notes an important difference between two versions of "Force of Law": the lecture as originally delivered at the Cardozo Law School in 1989, and the published version of 1994. In the original version, Derrida says: "I would hesitate to assimilate too quickly this 'idea of justice' to a regulative idea (in the Kantian sense), to a messianic promise or to other horizons of the same type."[36] But in the published version of 1994, Derrida amends his remarks: "I would hesitate to assimilate too quickly this 'idea of justice' to a regulative idea in the Kantian sense, to any content whatsoever of a messianic promise (I say *content* and not form, for every messianic form, every messianicity, is never absent from a promise, whatever it may be) or to other horizons of the same *type.*"[37]

Two important points must be stressed here. First, the idea of justice, which Derrida associates in the second version with "messianicity" (as opposed to a concrete "messianism"), is distinguished from a Kantian regulative idea. Second, Derrida makes a distinction between the form and the content of the messianic promise, and, so it seems, privileges form over content. Each of these points requires comment.

Derrida's reluctance to associate the idea of justice with the regulative idea in the Kantian sense results precisely from his desire to dissociate justice from an ideal toward which one can make progress but never fully attain. In *Rogues,* Derrida notes that his reservations with regard to the regulative idea are of three sorts—even though he says that he might one day give in to the regulative idea, which "retains a certain dignity."

The first reservation concerns the fact that the notion of a regulative idea is commonly employed—outside of its strict Kantian determination—to designate an ideal that is possible to obtain, though it is infinitely deferred. Justice or messianicity stands opposed to this regulative idea, precisely because it belongs to the order of the "impossible." Recall that while justice remains heterogeneous to the law, it nonetheless cannot exist without the law. Since the law necessarily compromises justice, justice as such is impossible, and the relationship between the law and justice is therefore an aporetic one. As I have argued, justice as respect for the singularity of the other is not prescribed by deconstruction as such; rather, deconstructive reading is undertaken, for Derrida, on account of an injunction that constitutes a desire for the impossible. This point is again confirmed here in *Rogues:* "This im-possible [. . .] comes upon me from on high, in the form of an injunction that does not simply wait on the horizon, that I do not see coming, that never leaves me in peace and never lets me put it off until later."[38]

Second, Derrida wishes to dissociate justice or messianicity from the regulative idea on account of the fact that the decisions one must make in the name of justice "cannot consist in following, applying, or carrying out a norm or a rule." This point follows from Derrida's argument in "Force of Law" to the effect that, since a decision involves not simply following a rule, but accounting for the singularity of the case, there is nothing that can assure one in advance of the justice of any decision (hence the "madness of decision"). Yet since a "regulative" idea is regulative precisely because it provides a guide toward the attainment of a particular end, justice cannot be a regulative idea. Finally, Derrida notes that he would be hesitant to employ the notion of the regulative idea because it cannot be so easily abstracted from its original Kantian context, intertwined as it is with the entire Kantian architectonic, to which he cannot wholly subscribe.[39] Indeed, Derrida has devoted many pages to interrogating and displacing this Kantian architectonic.

Justice and messianicity, then, are not regulative ideas. What about Derrida's curious distinction between the "form" and the "content" of the messianic promise? Form and content look suspiciously like concepts that Derrida would otherwise be inclined to deconstruct.[40] How, precisely, is one to understand this distinction? Is messianicity a "universal," as opposed to the particularity of the various historical, determinate messianisms? To answer this question, it is necessary to examine Derrida's discussion of messianicity in "Faith and Knowledge," and, in particular, the way in which this discussion of messianicity is framed as a transposition of the Kantian gesture of thinking "religion within the limits of reason alone."

VII

For Derrida, messianicity is linked to the "*coming of the other as the advent of justice.*" Since justice is strictly speaking "impossible," the object of this messianic expectation not only never arrives as such, but is also in principle heterogeneous to any concrete determination of what the messianic arrival would look like. Therefore, this messianicity is not reducible to a concrete messianism of the Christian, Jewish, Islamic, or even Marxist variety. Messianicity remains "*without horizon of expectation and without prophetic prefiguration.*" And since justice involves an experience of radical undecidability, where the justice of any decision can never be known before the decision itself, messianicity remains a fundamentally nonteleological notion, since no program or calculation can guarantee any closer proximity to justice. In fact, the radical unforseeability involved in this messianic desire means that it is an exposure to "radical evil" as much as it is the coming of justice: "*The messianic exposes itself to absolute surprise and, even if it always takes the phenomenal form of peace or of justice, it ought, exposing itself so abstractly, be prepared (waiting without awaiting* itself*) for the best as for the worst, the one never coming without opening the possibility of the other.*"[41]

Insofar as messianicity designates a "'*general structure of experience*'" in which one is always exposed to a future that is unforeseeable, this messianicity is in fact one of Derrida's oldest themes. In 1968, Derrida wrote that, from Parmenides to Husserl, "the privilege of the present has never been put into question," and that "the past and the future are always determined as past presents or as future presents."[42] What Derrida here calls "future presents" is what, in Husserlian terms, is called "protention," the anticipation of the future as a continuation of the present, a future that conforms to a horizon of expectation that is determined on the basis of the present. Over and against this notion of the future, Derrida argues that there is no experience of time without an irreducible exposure to the coming of that which breaks with the horizon of expectation. And in the exergue to *Of Grammatology,* Derrida speaks of this radical exposure to the future not in terms of the advent of justice, but in terms of the birth of the monstrous: "The future can only be anticipated in the form of an absolute danger. It is that which breaks absolutely with constituted normality and can only be proclaimed, *presented,* as a sort of monstrosity."[43] The reference to monstrosity is quite interesting here, since it stands in stark contrast to "justice." And yet, monstrosity is perhaps the more appropriate term, not because it bears any essential relation to the *content* of the future, which, while exposed to the necessary danger of being a monstrosity, might very well not be a monstrosity. But the "monstrous" has the advantage of capturing the notion of a future that breaks with the horizon of expectation. It does not partake of the "forms" that one can readily anticipate on the basis of the present, but is precisely a "deformity" in relation to the horizon of expectation.

What is at stake, then, in "messianicity," is not *simply* a general structure of experience, since the general structure of experience is no more linked with justice than it is with monstrosity. Messianicity no doubt involves this openness to a radical futurity, since without such openness there could be no experience in the first place. But what is added to this general structure of experience is a desire that has for its content justice as a "*universalizable culture of singularities, a culture in which the abstract possibility of the impossible translation could nevertheless be announced.*"[44]

For Derrida, it is this thought of messianicity that allows for a universal and rational discourse on religion, or in other words, allows one to transpose the Kantian gesture. But now the question of which "Kantian" gesture Derrida is in fact transposing becomes extremely pertinent. Is what Derrida has identified here under the term messianicity a genuinely universal structure? I have suggested that messianicity—which involves the notion of an exposure to a future that breaks with any horizon of expectation—can itself be considered universal, and that this aspect of Derrida's thought is certainly not a new development. However, the desire for justice (a universalizable culture of singularities) as the injunction that motivates Derrida's deconstructive analyses seems less generally universalizable, and certainly not foreign to the notions of Enlightenment and democracy to which Derrida professes an allegiance. What is important, however, is that Derrida in fact *calls into question the very claim to universality that he proffers under the name "messianicity."* And he does this by inscribing messianicity under the name of "reflective faith," a notion that itself deconstructs Kant's claim to have been able to demarcate the universal and rational form of religion from historical, dogmatic faith.

Recall, first of all, that reflective faith is situated parergonally between rational and dogmatic faith. In the *Religion,* this third kind of faith was necessitated by the fact that, on account of the impotence of reason to satisfy its moral needs, reason must transgress its own limits and touch upon transcendent questions. This faith that touches upon transcendent questions, and yet does not, like dogmatic faith, incorporate these transcendent ideas into its maxims, is precisely what Kant calls "reflective faith." And Kant insists that this activity, whereby reason goes beyond its boundaries to supplement its own internal lack, is a secondary or parergonal activity that is not properly a part of rational religion, but borders upon it.

Furthermore, following Derrida's analysis in "Faith and Knowledge" and "Parergon," this parergonal structure of reflective faith means that there is no universal, rational religion without exposure to that which threatens it, since this necessary transgression of the bounds of reason makes possible the various types of belief that threaten morality (enthusiasm, illumination, superstition, and thaumaturgy). Therefore, Kant is not, for Derrida, able to successfully police the border between the universal, rational religion and dogmatic faith.

With this in mind, let us return to the question of messianism. In a number of texts, Derrida draws attention to a difficulty embedded in the idea of messianicity and its relationship to determinate messianisms—a difficulty that raises the following question: Why does Derrida appeal to the language of the messianic at all, when it had previously been possible for him to describe what takes place under this notion without any specific reference to the religious messianisms? In "Marx & Sons," Derrida summarizes this difficulty as follows:

> I find it hard to decide whether messianicity without messianism (*qua* universal structure) precedes and conditions every determinate, historical figure of messianism (in which case it would be radically independent of all such figures, and would remain heterogeneous from them, making the name itself a matter of merely incidental interest), or whether the possibility of thinking this independence has only come about or revealed itself as such by way of the 'Biblical' events which name the messiah and make him a determinate figure.[45]

Thus Derrida hesitates here concerning the question of whether this reference to the messianic is ultimately dispensable—since it names something that precedes every determinate messianism—or whether there is an intrinsic link between messianicity and messianism, since such messianicity can be thought only by way of the concrete, biblical messianisms. In "Faith and Knowledge," this question is formulated in terms of the opposition between "revealability" (*Offenbarkeit*)—the name for a Heideggerian-type gesture that seeks to uncover the fundamental ontological structures that precede and make possible any specifically religious comportment—and "revelation" (*Offenbarung*)—the name for the Hegelian-type gesture in which the religious comportment or representation precedes the abstraction and universalization of this religious representation into a genuine philosophical universality. Derrida summarizes:

> *In its most abstract form, then, the aporia within which we are struggling would perhaps be the following: is revealability* (Offenbarkeit) *more originary than revelation* (Offenbarung), *and hence independent of all religion? Independent*

> *in the structures of its experience and the analytics relating to them? Is this not the place in which 'reflecting faith' at least originates, if not this faith itself? Or rather, inversely, would the event of revelation have consisted in revealing revealability itself, and the origin of light, the originary light, the very invisibility of visibility?*[46]

Derrida asks here whether reflective faith can be located on the side of revealability. But as we have seen, reflective faith is not simply situated on the side of universality in the Kantian text, but rather in the parergonal space that is neither properly inside rational religion nor outside of it. This question, then, is not a rhetorical one with a clearly implied answer.

Instead, the stakes of this question are very important for Derrida. If messianicity is a universalizing gesture that, in the manner of Kant, aims to think religion "within the limits of reason alone," it nevertheless remains that this supposed universality can only be thought on the basis of the "biblical messianisms." In fact, "biblical messianisms" may be too broad here, since, in fact, the attempt to universalize and rationalize a religious tradition, purged of its dogmatic content, is a fundamentally *Christian* gesture, as Derrida recognizes:

> *How then to think—within the limits of reason alone—a religion which, without again becoming 'natural religion', would today be effectively universal? And which, for that matter, would no longer be restricted to a paradigm that was Christian or even Abrahamic? What would be the project of such a 'book'? For with* Religion within the Limits of Reason Alone, *there is a World involved that is also an Old-New Book of Testament. Does this project retain a meaning or a chance? A geopolitical chance or meaning? Or does the idea itself remain, in its origin and in its end, Christian?*[47]

In other words, as Derrida suggests in "Marx & Sons," messianicity, if indeed it is only thinkable on the basis of determinate messianism, might itself be linked to "globalatinization."[48]

In "Marx & Sons," Derrida claims not to be able to *decide* whether messianicity represents a universal structure that precedes all determinate messianism, or whether messianicity remains thinkable only on the basis of messianism and therefore linked to it. But this indecision is not simply something negative, an attitude taken in the face of a lack of knowledge that might one day be supplied. In a crucial passage of "Faith and Knowledge," Derrida writes:

> *The indecisive oscillation, that reticence* (epoché *or* Verhaltenheit) *already alluded to above (between revelation and revealability,* Offenbarung *and* Of-

> fenbarkeit, *between event and possibility or virtuality of the event), must it not be respected for itself? Respect for this singular indecision or for this hyperbolic outbidding between two originarities, the order of the 'revealed' and the order of the 'revealable', is this not at once the chance of every responsible decision and of another 'reflecting faith, of a new 'tolerance'?*[49]

Kevin Hart's comment, that "rather than negotiate the difference between *Offenbarkeit* and *Offenbarung*, revealability and revelation, [Derrida] dogmatically affirmed the primacy of *Offenbarkeit*," could not be further from the truth.[50] Rather than being decided one way or another, the "indecisive oscillation" between revelation and revealability, Derrida says, must be kept open. The fact that this indecisive oscillation is linked to reticence or *Verhaltenheit* is significant, since it is a comportment of respect for the other that dictates this indecision. The universality of messianicity is therefore, in the final analysis, held in suspense. And just as reflective faith, according to Derrida's deconstructive reading of Kant's *Religion*, oscillates between the universal and the determinate, between rational and dogmatic faith, Derrida's transposition of this reflective faith consists not in drawing a rigorous line of demarcation between the universal and the determinate—and thereby repeating the classical logic of the fetish, positing a thing itself of religion as opposed to its substitutes—but in calling into question the universality of his own universalizing gesture. Indeed, this oscillation will remain, for Derrida, an interminable one, precisely because the object of the messianic desire—justice as a universal culture of singularities—remains impossible, always "to come," on account of the irreconcilable and non-sublatable tension between the universal (law) and the singular (justice).

With these points in mind, let us return to the "suspicious" formulation of the messianic that Derrida offers in "Force of Law," wherein Derrida posits a distinction between messianicity and messianism in terms of the distinction between "form" and "content": "I would hesitate to assimilate too quickly this 'idea of justice' to a regulative idea in the Kantian sense, to any content whatsoever of a messianic promise (I say *content* and not form, for every messianic form, every messianicity, is never absent from a promise, whatever it may be) or to other horizons of the same *type*."[51]

Since this messianicity aims at "justice," the impossible universal culture of singularities, it is not exactly without content, even if the object of this messianic desire remains heterogeneous to any determinate messianism. In this respect, Caputo is quite correct when he claims that Derrida's messianicity is "*one more* messianism, but one with a deconstructive twist," adding that a truly universal messianicity, "if there is one, would have the form of absolute *inhospitality*, of uninhabitability."[52] But the opposition between form and content is already disrupted by Derrida's claim that one must maintain the indecision between revelation (which would mean that messianicity remains historically determined) and revealability (which would make this messianicity an effectively universal structure). This indecision at least keeps in play the possibility that what seems to be only "form" (messianicity) may in fact already have a real, historically determined content. Derrida, therefore, is no doubt gesturing, like Kant, toward a universal religion or religiosity, and yet, by inscribing these reflections within the question of "reflective faith," he is—in the manner of another "Kant"—deconstructing his own universalizing gesture.

VIII

In keeping open the "indecisive oscillation" between revelation and revealability, Derrida says there is a chance for a "new tolerance." What, precisely, is the relationship between this "new tolerance" and tolerance as it is usually understood? For Derrida, tolerance remains a fundamentally Christian concept:

> *Let us suppose it agreed upon, among ourselves, that all of us here are for 'tolerance', even if we have not been assigned the mission of promoting it, practicing it or founding it. We would be here to try to think what 'tolerance' could henceforth be. I immediately place quotation marks around this word in order to abstract and extract it from its origins. And thereby to announce, through it, through the density of its history, a possibility that would not be solely Christian. For the concept of tolerance,* stricto sensu, *belongs first of all to a sort of Christian domesticity.*[53]

The concept of tolerance is born out of the religious wars that ravaged Europe, and is therefore a concept with a specifically Christian genealogy. Moreover, the idea of tolerance is intertwined with an Enlightenment discourse on religion that sought to distinguish, precisely, between that which is universal and rational in religion, and that which is purely historical and dogmatic. Tolerance, of course, emerges as a concept when mediation is sought between conflicting and competing interests, precisely through the appeal to certain universal categories that transcend individual differences. Therefore, tolerance embodies the very same tension between universality and singularity that we have now treated extensively by way of Derrida's opposition between law and justice.

The conceit of the Enlightenment discourse on tolerance was that it believed itself to have established universal categories that would make such mediation of alterity possible. Two points must be made about this conceit. First, since the generality of the universal (the law) necessarily stands in an antagonistic relationship to singularity, and therefore involves in various degrees the effacement of difference, then any form of tolerance will necessarily be violent. Second, this violence will not be violent to everyone, precisely because the universal itself is only the universalization of some particular interest or some particular singularity. Hence the concept of tolerance involves the raising of one particular, finite singularity, namely Christianity, to the level of universality. Derrida notes in "Faith and Knowledge" that even as anti-religious a thinker as Voltaire still holds to a discourse that exemplifies the Christian as the true bearer of tolerance:

> *The lesson of tolerance was first of all an exemplary lesson that the Christian deemed himself alone capable of giving to the world, even if he often had to learn it himself. In this respect, the French Enlightenment,* les Lumières, *was no less essentially Christian than the* Aufklärung. *When it treats of tolerance, Voltaire's* Philosophical Dictionary *reserves a dual privilege for the Christian religion. On the one hand it is exemplarily tolerant, to be sure, it teaches tolerance better than any other religion, before every other religion. In short, a little in the manner of Kant, believe it or not, Voltaire seems to think that Christianity is the sole 'moral' religion, since it is the first to feel itself obliged and capable of setting an example.* [. . .] [*But on*] *the other hand, the Voltairian lesson was addressed above all to Christians, 'the most intolerant of all men'. When Voltaire accuses the Christian religion and the Church, he invokes the lesson of originary Christianity, 'the times of the first Christians', Jesus and the Apostles, betrayed by 'the Catholic, Apostolic and Roman religion'. The latter is 'in all its ceremonies and in all its dogmas the opposite of the Religion of Jesus.'*[54]

Voltaire, Derrida suggests, makes a characteristic gesture, one that conforms to the "logic of the fetish": differentiating the true, originary Christianity (which is fundamentally linked to morality and tolerance) from its false substitute.

It should be said, however, that Derrida is quite uncharacteristically wide of the mark in his comments on Voltaire. Voltaire does indeed say that, of all religions, Christianity *should* instill the greatest toleration, though Christians have in fact proven themselves to be the most intolerant. The question, however, is whence comes this "should." Is it because, "a little in the manner of Kant," Voltaire believes Christianity to be the sole moral religion, as Derrida suggests? If Voltaire thinks so, he certainly does not say as much here; in fact, Voltaire says nothing about the ethical value of the teachings or practices of Jesus and the apostles in this entry of the *Philosophical Dictionary*. Rather, immediately following this comment, and no doubt by way of indirect explanation for the claim that Christianity should instill the greatest toleration, Voltaire writes: "Jesus having deigned to be born in poverty and a low condition, like his brothers, never condescended to practice the art of writing. The Jews had a legal system written down in the greatest detail, and we do not have a single line from the hand of Jesus. The apostles disagreed on a number of points."[55]

While Voltaire does not explicitly draw the connection, this juxtaposition of statements noting Jesus's failure to write anything down and disagreement between the apostles implies that the "originary Christianity," if we can speak of one, died with Jesus, leaving the apostles, and indeed all subsequent generations of Christians, to dispute amongst themselves concerning points of practice and doctrine. Voltaire points not only to Paul's rebuke of Peter's hypocrisy in Galatians 2:9–14, but also to Paul's own hypocrisy, witnessed by his willingness to perform, on the recommendation of James and the elders in Jerusalem, the Jewish ritual of purification in order to avoid the ire of those Jews who heard that he taught Jews in the Gentile world to turn their backs on the Mosaic Law (see Acts 21:18–26). Noting that Paul "judaized completely" during this episode, Voltaire adds: "For a week the greatest apostle of the Christians did the very things for which men are condemned to the stake by most Christian peoples." Then, noting both the sectarian nature of Judaism in the time of Jesus as well as the factiousness of the early Christians themselves, Voltaire concludes that "there has never been a single moment when the Christian Church was united," adding that "it was divided in its cradle."[56]

One finds in all of this an implied skepticism towards the ability to discern anything about the real teachings of Jesus from the New Testament writings themselves; and if one were to use the Gospels as a guide to recover the religion of Jesus, this religion would be nothing other than Judaism: "If it were permissible to reason consistently in matters of religion, it would become clear that we should all become Jews because our saviour Jesus Christ was born a Jew, lived a Jew, and died a Jew, and because he said expressly that he accomplished, that he fulfilled the Jewish religion."[57]

"Originary Christianity," to the extent that it has not been altogether lost, turns out to be Judaism. It is in this context that Voltaire makes the comment that Derrida refers to at the end of the passage from "Faith and Knowledge" quoted above: "If we look at the matter at all closely we see that the catholic, apostolic and Roman religion is the opposite of the religion of Jesus in all its ceremonies and in all its dogmas."[58] This contrast between the religion of Jesus and the dogmas of the Catholic Church bears no resemblance to the Kantian contrast between the pure moral religion and dogmatic or statutory faith; morality nowhere figures into Voltaire's remarks. Voltaire's point seems to be twofold: 1) the ceremonies and dogmas peculiar to Jesus are nothing other than the ceremonies and dogmas of Judaism; and 2) many of the ceremonies and dogmas of the Catholic Church are in no way those of Jesus and his disciples. (The Quakers, Voltaire notes, as he did some 30 years earlier in his *Philosophical Letters,* recall better than any other Christian sect the times of the first Christians—but even they did not "judaize" as thoroughly as Jesus "judaized.")

For Voltaire, then, Christians should be exemplarily tolerant because they are exemplarily prone to error, as proven by their factiousness, a factiousness that was present, as we have seen, from the very beginning. Voltaire writes: "We know that every sect is a guarantee of error. There are no sects of geometricians, algebraists, arithmeticians, because all the propositions of geometry, algebra, arithmetic are true. We can make mistakes in every other science. What Thomist or Scotist would dare to say seriously that he is sure of what he says?" The Christian, it seems, has at least as much, if not more reason than anyone else to adopt an attitude of skepticism concerning the various competing truth-claims of the sects of Christianity; and it is out of the recognition of our proneness to error that toleration, for Voltaire, finds its ultimate justification. After his comment, quoted above, that reasoning consistently in matters of religion would have all Christians living like Jews, he concludes the dictionary entry with the following lines: "But it is even clearer that we should tolerate each other because we are all weak, inconsistent, subject to mutability, and to error. Would a reed laid into the mud by the wind say to a neighboring reed bent in the opposite direction: 'Creep in my fashion, wretch, or I shall petition to have you torn up and burned?'"[59] In the end, one can only read Voltaire's assertion that Christianity should instill the greatest toleration as a backhanded compliment.

Nevertheless, Derrida's hesitation concerning the idea of toleration is very much on target for Kant. If Christianity provides the ground upon which a discourse on tolerance can be erected, it nevertheless remains that this was a certain Enlightenment interpretation of Christianity. This understanding divided all religion into "inner" and "outer" religion, a distinction corresponding to universality and particularity, rationality and enthusiasm, and morality and immorality.[60] Indeed, Kant's deployment of just such a binary logic in the *Religion* is precisely what makes possible, for Kant, a discourse on tolerance. In a footnote in Part III of the *Religion,* Kant writes:

> In spite of the diversity of statutory forms of faith, we can establish tolerance among their adherents through the basic principles of the one religion of reason, with reference to which teachers ought to expound all the dogmas and observances of their various faiths; until, with time, by virtue of a true enlightenment (an order of law originating in moral freedom) which has gained the upper hand, the form of a degrading means of compulsion can be exchanged, with everybody's consent, for an ecclesiastical form commensurate to the dignity of a moral religion, viz. a free faith.[61]

Tolerance can only be established among the various historical, determinate faiths via a genuine principle of universality, which can only be supplied by *one* such faith: Christianity. Therefore one singular faith among various singular faiths is elevated to a universality in which, ironically enough, none of these other faiths partake, insofar as Christianity remains, Kant insists, the *sole* moral religion.

It is to be expected that the modern Christian-philosophical tradition should have elevated this moral interpretation of Christianity to a universal principle, since it was precisely Christian infighting in the wake of the Protestant Reformation and the subsequent Wars of Religion that gave rise to a theorization of the concept of tolerance. And yet, as Derrida notes, this concept of tolerance continues to be applied to a discourse on religion and religious conflict today, when such conflict is no longer just a case of Christian against Christian, but involves traditions alien to the particular European context in which the concept of tolerance was developed.

Derrida employs the term "globalatinization" (*mondialatinisation*) to refer to the hegemonic process whereby, allied with capitalism and the resources of tele-technology, the Christian discourse on religion exports itself to every corner of the globe, justifying this hegemony precisely on the basis of a belief in the universality of Christianity. This globalatinization, according to Derrida, belongs not simply to the concept of tolerance, but extends to the very concept of "religion" itself.

> Does not 'the question of *religio*', however, quite simply merge, one could say, with the question of Latin? By which should be understood, beyond a 'question of language and culture', the strange phenomenon of Latinity and of its globalization. We are not speaking here of universality, even of an idea of universality, only of a process of uni-

> versalization that is finite but enigmatic. It is rarely investigated in its geopolitical and ethico-juridical scope, precisely where such a power finds itself overtaken, deployed, its *paradoxical* heritage revived by the global and still irresistible hegemony of a 'language', which is to say, also of a culture that in part is not Latin but Anglo-American. For everything that touches religion in particular, for everything that speaks 'religion', for whoever speaks religiously or about religion, Anglo-American remains Latin. *Religion* circulates in the world, one might say, like an *English word* <*comme un mot anglais*> that has been to Rome and taken a detour to the United States. Well beyond its strictly capitalist or politico-military figures, a hyper-imperialist appropriation has been underway now for centuries. It imposes itself in a particularly palpable manner within the conceptual apparatus of international law and of global political rhetoric. Whenever this apparatus dominates, it articulates itself through a discourse on religion. From here on, the word 'religion' is calmly (and violently) applied to things which have always been and remain foreign to what this word names and arrests in its history. The same remark could apply to many other words, [to] the entire 'religious vocabulary' beginning with 'cult', 'faith', 'belief', 'sacred', 'holy', 'saved', 'unscathed' (*heilig*). But by ineluctable contagion, no semantic cell can remain alien, I dare not say 'safe and sound', 'unscathed', in this apparently borderless process. *Globalatinization* (essentially Christian, to be sure), this word names a unique event to which a meta-language seems incapable of acceding, although such a language remains, all the same, of the greatest necessity here.[62]

It is striking that the words which Derrida says belong to the religious vocabulary of the Christian West—and which are therefore part and parcel of the hegemonic process of globalatinization—are the very same words he employs throughout "Faith and Knowledge" in his attempt to determine a universal structure of religiosity. This is no doubt dictated for Derrida by the fact that, as he says, globalatinization is an event for which there is no meta-language, no point of access that is not in some way already appropriated or governed by the discourse of globalatinization.

The fact that Derrida employs the very language of the tradition he seeks to deconstruct is, of course, the most characteristic of deconstructive strategies. Just as there is no stepping outside the language of metaphysics or ontology (which is perhaps the primary lesson, demonstrated both against and with Levinas, of "Violence and Metaphysics"), so too there is no stepping outside the Christian religious vocabulary that has governed every relation to the non-Western and non-Christian. Derrida's deconstruction of this hegemony, therefore, is carried out within the very terms of this tradition, and therefore in Kantian terms, as Kant remains an exemplary figure within this tradition.

Kant is exemplary precisely on account of his attempt not simply to identify morality with Christianity—an identification which no doubt was made before Kant—but, rather, in tandem with his destruction of philosophical theology, to make morality the *sole point of access* for any philosophical engagement with religion. This enabled Kant to offer not simply a universal and rationalistic approach to the idea of God, but also a rationalistic approach to religious symbols, institutions, and history. This approach is clearly not without its aporias and paradoxes, given the fact that religious history threatens the very morality it is supposed to promote. Nevertheless, Kant's *Religion* is one of the most powerful attempts to unite Christianity and morality in a universalistic and triumphalist discourse. It is thus no surprise that Kant should be the decisive point of reference for Derrida in "Faith and Knowledge."

What is surprising, however (at least for Derrida's critics) is the degree to which his later texts, including "Force of Law" and "Faith and Knowledge," maintain a fidelity to the Enlightenment heritage generally, and to the Kantian heritage specifically. Derrida, as we have seen, casts his lot with what he calls

> *an unreserved taste, if not an unconditional preference, for what, in politics, is called republican democracy as a universalizable model, binding philosophy to the public 'cause', to the* res publica, *to 'public-ness', once again to the light of day, once again to the 'lights' of the Enlightenment* <aux Lumières>, *once again to the enlightened virtue of public space, emancipating it from all external power (non-lay, non-secular), for example from religious dogmatism, orthodoxy or authority (that is, from a certain rule of the* doxa *or of belief, which, however, does not mean from all faith).*[63]

No doubt, this commitment to the Enlightenment heritage extends to the notion of tolerance. But if this tolerance remains a fundamentally Christian and therefore hegemonic concept, one that respects the other only by way of a certain violence, then this tolerance remains to be thought otherwise: "*Another 'tolerance' would* [. . .] *respect the distance of infinite alterity as singularity. And this respect would still be* religio, religio *as scruple or reticence, distance, dissociation, disjunction, coming from the threshold of all religion in the* link of repetition to itself, *the threshold of every social or communitarian link.*"[64] A true commitment to this Enlightenment heritage, for Derrida, ultimately involves a vigilant and deconstructive interrogation of this tradition in the name of the impossible unconditionality that goes by the various names of justice, hospitality, messianicity, and the democracy to come. Derrida thus speaks, in *Rogues,* of an "Enlightenment to come":

> For deconstruction, if something of the sort exists, would remain above all, in my view, an unconditional rationalism that never renounces—and precisely in the name of the Enlightenment to come, in the space to be opened up of a democracy to come—the possibility of suspending in an argued, deliberated, rational fashion, all conditions, hypotheses, conventions, and presuppositions, and of criticizing unconditionally all conditionalities, including those that still found the critical idea, namely, those of the *krinein,* of the *krisis,* of the binary or dialectical decision or judgment.[65]

An allegiance to the Enlightenment means deconstructing the Enlightenment tradition right down to its foundational concepts in the name of an Enlightenment to come, even if this Enlightenment to come remains, strictly speaking, impossible, and therefore never arrives. This, then, is the precise meaning of the "Kantian transposition." Kant's gesture of thinking religion "within the limits of reason alone" is not, for Derrida, something to be rejected, nor is it something to be *simply repeated.* "Transposing the Kantian gesture" signifies, as I have shown, precisely the repetition of a "certain Kant," one whose own universalizing gesture is deconstructed in its very pretension to universality.

Conclusion

I would like in conclusion to articulate what I take to be the significance of Derrida's engagement with Kant's philosophy of religion. I began this book with the suggestion that continental philosophy of religion in the twentieth century was in an important way a repetition of philosophy of religion in the eighteenth, for two reasons. The first is the failure (real or perceived) of traditional metaphysics and philosophical theology; the second is the attempt to rethink God and religion, in the wake of this failure, by way of ethics. Whether Derrida would have conceived things in these terms, I cannot claim to know. It is significant, however, that when Derrida asks what it would mean to think religion *today*, he describes this attempt as a transposition of the Kantian gesture of thinking religion within the limits of reason alone.

Of course, when Derrida speaks of the "Kantian gesture," it is a matter of knowing, as I have argued, precisely to which "Kant" Derrida is referring. It is for this reason that much of this book is devoted to a close reading of Derrida's various engagements with both Kant's ethics and his philosophy of religion. As is to be expected, these readings have demonstrated the quasi-transcendental nature of Kant's ethics and his philosophy of religion. Therefore, the Kantian gesture that is transposed in "Faith and Knowledge" is one in which "religion within the limits of reason alone" finds itself constitutively and unavoidably contaminated by that which threatens it.

In Chapter 1, I argued that Kant's theology is *spectral.* While ethics must be able to survive the death of God, the God resurrected by practical reason must never come back fully to life, lest one act out of fear of the living God rather than out of respect for the moral law; such is the price of construing God as an idea of practical reason. Further, I argued that Kant's hermeneutic project consists, first and foremost, in an attempt to bring religion within the scope of practical reason by checking the tendency of Christianity, the sole moral religion, to degenerate into counterfeit service and fetishism; that Kant was unsuccessful in insulating the thing itself of moral religion from such fetishism is the crux of Derrida's engagement with the *Religion.* I have suggested, however, that the truth of Kant's philosophy of religion is that the idea of God is a strictly *anthropological* one, and that the tension in Kant's *Religion* really derives from the nature of the human being as a finite and sensible (albeit rational) being. Therefore, if fetishism remains inescapable, it is precisely on account of this human finitude.

Because of the specific objective of this book, I have not engaged the question of whether Derrida is a religious thinker, or whether Derrida's thought provides the means for constructing a post-metaphysical or postmodern theology. But since a number of Derrida's texts on religion have been at the center of my discussion, perhaps it will be helpful to say a few words about this. As for using Derrida's texts for the construction of a postmodern theology, I indicated in the introduction that one of the basic lessons of deconstruction is the inevitable susceptibility of these texts, and indeed any text, to all kinds of appropriation and expropriation. Nevertheless, I do not take it to have been Derrida's purpose to construct such a theology, and by examining the place of Kant in "Faith and Knowledge" and framing this engagement with Kant as an interrogation of the meaning and possibility of *philosophy of religion,* I have tried to open up a different way of thinking about Derrida's late texts.

Whether Derrida himself was a religious thinker depends entirely upon how one understands the word "religious." I therefore find this question rather impossible to answer, simply because it would require us to know what "religion" is, and what "God" means; but as we see in the merry-go-round staged in *Glas* among Kant, Freud, and Hegel, it is precisely the meaning of "God" and the meaning of "religion" that is in question. So to classify or de-classify Derrida in this way would require joining the merry-go-round and positing a thing itself of religion.

In fact, one cannot simply refuse to join the merry-go-round; one is already on it. For however much Derrida seems to observe this staged encounter between Kant, Freud, and Hegel from the outside, Derrida is himself a part of it. This is clear, above all, in "Faith and Knowledge," where Derrida's reticence in the face of the question of religion results not in a refusal to respond, but rather in the response that "religion is the response." Of course, as I have attempted to show, by inscribing his entire discourse in "Faith and Knowledge" under the banner of "reflective faith," Derrida is transposing Kant in a way that attempts to keep open the play between revealability and revelation, between a truly transcendental religiosity and a determinate, historical religion. Here, the distinction between "philosopher of religion" in the Kantian model—one who thinks a religion of pure reason free from the historical—and one who is simply a "religious thinker," thinking from within a given religious heritage, becomes undecidable. As we have seen, "Faith and Knowledge" deliberately keeps this undecidability in play, rather than conforming to the "classic logic of the fetish."

It is significant, of course, that Derrida utilizes the words "religion," "faith," "holiness," "messianicity," "sacrifice," and any number of other concepts that derive from the religious and theological heritage. This is to be expected; another of the basic lessons of deconstruction is that one does not step outside of this heritage, but thinks within it and displaces it only by utilizing the very resources bequeathed by it. Whether the mere occurrence of these terms, then, is enough to identify Derrida as a "religious" thinker depends upon whether one believes that these concepts have been too significantly displaced to have any significant relation to those same terms in any of their previous meanings. The history of religious and philosophical thought is simply the history of these displacements, displacements that are proffered and then accepted, rejected, or further displaced in the belief that one can eliminate the fetish and identify the thing itself of religion. It is likely that readers of Derrida will continue to fight for some time over the religious interpretation/appropriation of Derrida's writings—Hägglund's insistence on Derrida's "radical atheism" will certainly not be the end to such debate—but this merry-go-round will only vindicate Derrida's very diagnosis of the so-called "philosophy of religion."

Abbreviations

In the notes to this volume, works by Jacques Derrida and Immanuel Kant have been cited using the following abbreviations. All references to Kant's texts are given according to the standard Prussian Academy Edition pagination; quotations are taken from the translations listed below.

Works by Jacques Derrida

AD *Adieu: To Emmanuel Levinas.* Translated by Pascale-Anne Brault and Michael Naas. Stanford: Stanford University Press, 1999.

BL "Before the Law." In *Acts of Literature.* Edited by Derek Attridge. Translated by Christine Roulston, 181–220. New York: Routledge, 1992.

DF "Différance." In *Margins of Philosophy.* Translated by Alan Bass, 1–27. Chicago: University of Chicago Press, 1982.

DI "Declarations of Independence." *New Political Science* 15 (1986): 7–15.

DM *Dissemination.* Translated by Barbara Johnson. Chicago: The University of Chicago Press, 1981.

EM "Economimesis." Translated by Richard Klein. *Diacritics* 11 (1981): 2–25.

EN "The Ends of Man." In *Margins of Philosophy.* Translated by Alan Bass, 109–36. Chicago: University of Chicago Press, 1982.

FK "Faith and Knowledge: The Two Sources of 'Religion' at the Limits of Reason Alone." In *Religion.* Edited by Jacques Derrida and Gianni Vattimo. Translated by Samuel Weber, 1–78. Stanford: Stanford University Press, 1998.

FL "Force of Law: The 'Mystical Foundation of Authority.'" In *Acts of Religion.* Edited by Gil Anidjar. Translated by Mary Quaintance, 230–98. New York: Routledge, 2002.

FM "Form and Meaning: A Note on the Phenomenology of Language." In *Margins of Philosophy*. Translated by Alan Bass, 155–73. Chicago: The University of Chicago Press, 1982.

GD *The Gift of Death*. Translated by David Wills. Chicago: The University of Chicago Press, 1995.

GL *Glas*. Translated by John P. Leavey Jr. and Richard Rand. Lincoln: University of Nebraska Press,1986.

GR *Of Grammatology*. Translated by Gayatri Chakravorty Spivak. Baltimore: The Johns Hopkins University Press, 1997.

HL "History of the Lie: Prolegomena." In *Futures: Of Jacques Derrida*. Edited by Richard Rand. Translated by Peggy Kamuf, 65–98. Stanford: Stanford University Press, 2001.

LI *Limited Inc*. Edited by Gerald Graff. Evanston: Northwestern University Press, 1988.

LJ "Letter to a Japanese Friend." In *Derrida and* Différance. Edited by David Wood and Robert Bernasconi. Translated by David Wood and Andrew Benjamin, 1–5. Evanston: Northwestern University Press, 1988.

MS "Marx & Sons." In *Ghostly Demarcations: A Symposium on Jacques Derrida's* Specters of Marx. Edited by Michael Sprinkler. Translated by G. M. Goshgarian, 213–69. New York: Verso, 2008.

OG *Edmund Husserl's* Origin of Geometry: *An Introduction by Jacques Derrida*. Translated by John P. Leavey Jr. Lincoln: University of Nebraska Press, 1978.

OH *Of Hospitality: Anne Dufourmantelle Invites Jacques Derrida to Respond*. Translated by Rachel Bowlby. Stanford: Stanford University Press, 2000.

OU "*Ousia* and *Grammē*: Note on a Note from *Being and Time*." In *Margins of Philosophy*. Translated by Alan Bass, 29–67. Chicago: University of Chicago Press, 1982.

PF *The Politics of Friendship*. Translated by George Collins. New York: Verso, 2005.

PM *Paper Machine*. Translated by Rachel Bowlby. Stanford: Stanford University Press, 2005.

PS "Passions: 'An Oblique Offering.'" In *On the Name*. Edited by Thomas Dutoit. Translated by David Wood, 3–31. Stanford: Stanford University Press, 1995.

PT — *Philosophy in a Time of Terror: Dialogues with Jürgen Habermas and Jacques Derrida.* Edited by Giovanna Borradori. Chicago: The University of Chicago Press, 2003.

RP — "Réligion et philosophie." Jacques Derrida Papers. MS-C01. Special Collections and Archives, The UC Irvine Libraries, Irvine, California. Box 11, Folders 14–19. Lecture notes from a seminar given in 1972–73.

RR — *Rogues: Two Essays on Reason.* Translated by Pascale-Anne Brault and Michael Naas. Stanford: Stanford University Press, 2005.

SE — "Signature Event Context." In *Margins of Philosophy.* Translated by Alan Bass, 307–30. Chicago: University of Chicago Press, 1982.

SP — *Speech and Phenomena.* Translated by David B. Allison. Evanston: Northwestern University Press, 1973.

SS — "Structure, Sign, and Play in the Discourse of the Human Sciences." In *Writing and Difference.* Translated by Alan Bass, 278–93. Chicago: The University of Chicago Press, 1978.

TP — *Truth in Painting.* Translated by Geoff Bennington and Ian McLeod. Chicago: The University of Chicago Press, 1987.

UG — "Ulysses Gramophone: Hear Say Yes in Joyce." In *Acts of Literature.* Edited by Derek Attridge. Translated by Tina Kendall and Shari Benstock, 253–309. New York: Routledge, 1992.

VM — "Violence and Metaphysics: An Essay on the Thought of Emmanuel Levinas." In *Writing and Difference.* Translated by Alan Bass, 79–153. Chicago: The University of Chicago Press, 1978.

WA — *Who's Afraid of Philosophy?: Right to Philosophy I.* Translated by Jan Plug. Stanford: Stanford University Press, 2002.

WT — *For What Tomorrow . . . A Dialogue.* With Elisabeth Roudinesco. Translated by Jeff Fort. Stanford: Stanford University Press, 2004.

Works by Immanuel Kant

CF — *The Conflict of the Faculties.* In *Religion and Rational Theology.* Edited by Allen W. Wood and George di Giovanni. Translated by Allen W. Wood. New York: Cambridge University Press, 1996.

CPJ *Critique of the Power of Judgment.* Edited by Paul Guyer. Translated by Paul Guyer and Eric Matthews. New York: Cambridge University Press, 2000.

CPrR *Critique of Practical Reason.* In *Practical Philosophy.* Edited and translated by Mary J. Gregor. New York: Cambridge University Press, 1996.

CPR *Critique of Pure Reason.* Edited and translated by Paul Guyer and Allen W. Wood. New York: Cambridge University Press, 1998.

GW *Groundwork of the Metaphysics of Morals.* In *Practical Philosophy.* Edited and translated by Mary J. Gregor. New York: Cambridge University Press, 1996.

LPR *Lectures on the Philosophical Doctrine of Religion.* In *Religion and Rational Theology.* Edited by Allen W. Wood and George di Giovanni. Translated by Allen W. Wood. New York: Cambridge University Press, 1996.

MM *Metaphysics of Morals.* In *Practical Philosophy.* Edited and translated by Mary J. Gregor. New York: Cambridge University Press, 1996.

MPT "On the Miscarriage of All Philosophical Trials in Theodicy." In *Religion and Rational Theology.* Edited by Allen W. Wood and George di Giovanni. Translated by George di Giovanni. New York: Cambridge University Press, 1996.

RL *Religion within the Boundaries of Mere Reason.* In *Religion and Rational Theology.* Edited by Allen W. Wood and George di Giovanni. Translated by George di Giovanni. New York: Cambridge University Press, 1996.

SRL "On a Supposed Right to Lie from Philanthropy." In *Practical Philosophy.* Edited and translated by Mary J. Gregor. New York: Cambridge University Press, 1996.

Notes

Introduction

EPIGRAPH: Nancy, *L'impératif catégorique,* 59, quoted in Fenves, review of *L'impératif catégorique,* 1136.

1. FK, 8, italics in the original.

2. WA, 50.

3. WA, 49.

4. Naas, *Miracle and Machine,* 6.

5. Ibid., 310.

6. For a thorough overview of such literature, see Shakespeare, *Derrida and Theology,* chapter 7.

Chapter 1

1. Jaeschke, *Reason in Religion,* 2.

2. Ibid., 3.

3. Ibid., 3–4. Jean Greisch notes that the first known use of the phrase "philosophy of religion" is by Sigismund von Storchenau (1731–1797), a Jesuit and Wolffian philosopher who published a *Philosophie der Religion* in 1772 (expanded to seven volumes over the years 1773–1781). This title was probably inspired by A. F. Ruckersfelder's *Philosophia de religione naturali* (1770). Nevertheless, as Greisch writes, the contents of this work conformed to the classic natural theology, with the apologetic intent of defending Catholicism as the true religion. Consequently, Greisch claims that the true philosophical profile of the "philosophy of religion" takes form with Karl Reinhold's *Letters on the Kantian Philosophy* (1786–1787). This would largely conform to Jaeschke's historical conclusions. See Greisch, *Le Buisson ardent,* 31.

4. This is also the position of Louis Dupré. Unlike Jaeschke, Dupré does not follow the fate of Kant's ethicotheology as such, but rather claims that, after restricting reliable theoretical knowledge to the phenomenal sphere, thereby precluding any claims of theoretical knowledge concerning the transcendent, "Kant left no avenue open to the religious object but that of experience itself." *A Dubious Heritage,* 4. Consequently, for Dupré, the fundamental challenge that Kant bequeathed to all subsequent attempts to think religion philosophically was to find out how theoretical support for God's existence could be demonstrated on the basis of experience alone, and how that experience could be "legitimated within the context of human autonomy." Ibid., 3. Thus Dupré's study of the philosophy of religion after Kant begins with Schleiermacher, and traces this prob-

lematic into the work of Husserl, Blondel, and Duméry. James Collins, on the other hand, in *The Emergence of Philosophy of Religion,* makes his beginning not with Kant, but with Hume. Hume was no doubt a central figure in the religious controversies of Kant's time, and Hamann and Jacobi exploited his writings to great effect. For the place of Hume in these religious controversies, see Beiser, *The Fate of Reason,* 89–91, as well as di Giovanni, "Introduction." It nevertheless remains that while Hume—at least according to Jaeschke's criteria—no doubt interpreted religion and the philosophical justifications for it in light of his own empiricist philosophy, it was never his project to establish a "philosophy of religion" as such.

5. Jaeschke, *Reason in Religion,* 4–5.

6. For a detailed examination of Kant's treatment of the traditional proof for the existence of God in the first *Critique* and beyond it, see Wood, *Kant's Rational Theology.*

7. Jaeschke, *Reason in Religion,* 5.

8. "Now let us ask: what is the minimum of theology required for religion? What is the smallest useful cognition of God that can accordingly move us to have faith in God and thus direct our course of life? What is the smallest, narrowest concept of theology? It is that we need a religion, and that the concept is sufficient for natural religion. There is this minimum, however, if I see that my concept of God is *possible* and that it does not contradict the laws of the understanding.—Can everyone be convinced of this much? Yes, everyone can, because no one is in a position to rob us of this concept and prove that it is impossible. Hence this is the smallest possible requirement for a religion. Provided that this alone is made a ground, there can always be religion." LPR, 28:998.

9. Kant goes on, in the same passage, to say that this possible God "is not the maximum of theology. It would be better if I knew that such a being actually existed." Ibid., 28:998–99.

10. CPrR, 5:146.

11. CPrR, 5:147.

12. "Natural morality must be so constituted that it can be thought independently of any concept of God, and obtain zealous reverence from us solely on account of its own inner dignity and excellence." LPR, 28:1002–1003.

13. CPrR, 5:110.

14. CPR, A 806/B 834.

15. CPrR, 5:111.

16. Kant says that two Greek schools, the Stoics and the Epicureans, maintained the identity of virtue and happiness. "The Epicurean said: to be conscious of one's maxim leading to happiness is virtue; the Stoic said: to be conscious of one's virtue is happiness." CPrR, 5:111. Kant regrets that the "acuteness of these men" was applied to seeking the identity of virtue and happiness, which are in fact "extremely heterogeneous concepts." Ibid.

17. CPrR, 5:113.

18. Ibid., 5:113–14.

19. Guyer, "From a Practical Point of View," 351. Guyer sees a tacit acknowledgement of this point in the fact that, while Kant lumps the three postu-

lates together in the second *Critique* (as in section concerning the "Postulates of Pure Practical Reason in General" [5:132]), he only provides a detailed analysis of God and immortality. This is not, of course, to deny that freedom, for Kant, is postulated rather than known theoretically. It is simply to make a qualitative distinction between those postulates that are required for the attainment of the highest good (the failure of which does not compromise the validity of the moral principle), and the postulation of freedom, without which the notion of an unconditionally binding moral law would be invalidated.

20. CPrR, 5:122.

21. Guyer, "From a Practical Point of View," 352.

22. Proof of the fact that a holy will does not, according to Kant's own arguments, aim at the satisfaction of inclinations can be found in the *Groundwork of the Metaphysics of Morals*. There Kant writes, concerning happiness: "There is, however, *one* end that can be presupposed as actual in the case of all rational beings (insofar as imperatives apply to them, namely as dependent beings), and therefore one purpose that they not merely *could* have but that we can safely presuppose they all actually *do have* by a natural necessity, and that purpose is *happiness*." GW, 4:415. The key here is what Kant says in the parenthesis. Happiness can only be supposed to be the end of rational beings insofar as *imperatives apply to them*. But Kant asserts, just one page before this remark, that imperatives do not apply to a holy will: "A perfectly good will would, therefore, equally stand under objective laws (of the good), but it could not on this account be represented as *necessitated* to actions in conformity with the law since of itself, by its subjective constitution, it can be determined only through the representation of the good. Hence no imperatives hold for the *divine* will and in general for a *holy* will: the 'ought' is out of place here, because the volition is of itself necessarily in accord with the law. Therefore imperatives are only formulae expressing the relation of objective laws of volition in general to the subjective imperfection of the will of this or that rational being, for example, of the human will." GW, 4:414. It is clear therefore that, on Kant's own terms, speaking of a holy will that has happiness for its end is an absurdity.

23. Kant has a subsidiary concern in offering this argument for immortality as a postulate of practical reason. The claim that the moral law demands holiness of the will is intended to ensure that the law does not seem lenient in any way. But at the same time, Kant is concerned not to strain "one's calling as well as one's expectation to an unattainable vocation." CPrR, 5:122. The postulate of immortality, it seems, enables Kant to avoid both horns of this dilemma (leniency and unattainability). But holiness of the will for a finite rational being who can never be free of sensibility and therefore free of inclination is not simply a stringent demand, but a strictly impossible one. And this will continue to be the case for however long the life of this being extends, so long as the being remains finite and sensible. Therefore, immortality provides no real solution to this difficulty anyhow.

24. Jaeschke, *Reason in Religion*, 52.

25. CPrR, 5:125.

26. Ibid.

27. CPR, A 815/B 843.

28. CPrR, 5:125.

29. Ibid., 5:114.

30. This is Jaeschke's interpretation of Kant's argument as it stands in the second *Critique;* see Jaeschke, *Reason in Religion,* 57.

31. Allen Wood confirms this point; see Wood, *Kant's Moral Religion,* 25–27. While Jaeschke's interpretation of God as necessary for the validity of the moral law is an incorrect one with regard to the second *Critique,* it is the correct interpretation of Kant's views in the "Canon of Pure Reason" in the first *Critique,* where Kant offers his first formulation of his ethicotheology. After arguing for the necessity of God's existence for the possibility of the realization of the highest good, Kant writes: "Morality in itself constitutes a system, but happiness does not, except insofar as it is distributed precisely in accordance with morality. This, however, is possible only in the intelligible world, under a wise author and regent. Reason sees itself as compelled either to assume such a thing, together with life in such a world, which we must regard as a future one, or else to regard the moral laws as empty figments of the brain, since without that presupposition their necessary success, which the same reason connects with them, would have to disappear." CPR, A 811/B 839. The validity of the moral law, then, according to the stage of Kant's thinking represented in the first *Critique,* does risk becoming a "figment of the brain" without the postulation of God. Förster shows that Kant first came to realize the difficulty with this formulation as a result of Christian Garve's criticisms in his review of the first *Critique.* According to Hamann's letters, Kant began working on a response to Garve's criticisms and to Garve's newly published *Philosophische Anmerkungen und Abhandlungen zu Ciceros Büchern von den Pflichten,* but this response ultimately turned into the *Groundwork,* in which no direct reference to Garve was made. See Förster, *Kant's Final Synthesis,* 122–12.

32. GW, 4:414.

33. CPJ, 5:450–51.

34. Ibid., 5:462–63.

35. The entire thrust of this reading is confirmed by Guyer, who argues, on the basis of the full range of Kant's texts, that the postulates respond to the specific psychological makeup of humans as composed of both rational and sensible natures. He argues that for Kant, while the assurance of the noncontradictoriness of an end is all that is required to make the pursuit of that end rational, "human psychology is such that in fact it needs a greater incentive, a positive reason to believe its end is realizable [. . .] [T]o accommodate that feature of human psychology we can ourselves introduce and then act under the ideas of positive grounds for the reality of the highest good as well as under theoretical proof of its noncontradictoriness." Guyer, "From a Practical Point of View," 364–65. This leads Guyer to conclude that "the entire doctrine of the postulates of practical reason is stated within the limits of human psychology," and ultimately to understand Kant's ethicotheology as standing "alongside his aesthetics as an essential part of the moral anthropology that was the heart of his enterprise throughout his last decade of philosophical activity." Ibid., 367, 371. It is thus no accident, he claims, that Kant's "most detailed statement of his moral theology

is the culmination of the 'Critique of Teleological Judgment,' just as his most extensive statement of his moral aesthetics is the culmination of the 'Critique of Aesthetic Judgment.'" (Ibid, 371). For Guyer, however, as opposed to Jaeschke, the anthropological origin of the postulates is not seen as a limitation of Kant's theory, precisely because Guyer is not concerned with the question of the possibility of philosophy of religion as a philosophical discipline independent of speculative theology. But from the perspective of the founding of a philosophy of religion, the anthropological nature of this ethicotheology is detrimental, since it fails, thereby, to fill the void left by Kant's destruction of speculative theology, and ultimately leads to the conclusion that, in Jaeschke's words, "the idea of God is a complement of human weakness." Jaeschke, *Reason in Religion*, 81. Without having speculative theology to establish God's existence, "philosophy of religion" "has no choice but to regard religion generally as a manifestation of the human, from the point of view of social behavior or certain psychic effects. Any intention to confer on the divine a status other than human requires a philosophical theology, however rudimentary, not even necessarily elaborated as a separate discipline. Failing this, God necessarily becomes a human product or even the essence of human being; and this is no less the case if a philosophy of religion methodically seeks to bracket the problem of God. Unless it can adduce reasons for including God in the totality of possible objects of philosophy, there is no justification for attributing to the idea of God in one domain of philosophy, the philosophy of religion, any meaning other than that what is involved here is a particular kind of expression of human life. And a philosophy of religion that aims to adopt the standpoint of Protagoras and methodologically bracket the question of God is wide open to criticism from the side of a determinedly anthropological conception of religion. For even the hypothesis of an *anima naturaliter religiosa* (albeit no longer *christiana*) is quite compatible with the anthropological reduction of religion and even with the interpretation of religion as a collective neurosis; principally it makes clear that for this very reason religion is best suited, perhaps even indispensable, for overcoming the contingencies of life." Ibid., 7–8.

36. This would lend some credence to the organization of Greisch's three-volume study of the philosophy of religion, *Le Buisson ardent et les Lumières de la raison*. In this study, Greisch does not proceed chronologically, but rather organizes the history of the philosophy of religion in accordance with five different paradigms of reason, which are not meant to be exclusive and rigorous, but are used heuristically. These paradigms of reason are speculative, "critical," phenomenological, analytic, and hermeneutic. What is interesting here is that Greisch divides the critical paradigm in two; critical reason in the philosophy of religion refers on the one hand to Kant and his successors (Hermann Cohen, Ernst Troeltsch, Paul Tillich, and Henry Duméry), and on the other to the "anthropological critiques" of religion in Feuerbach and Nietzsche. In the first case, critical reason refers precisely to Kant's notion of critique, establishing the limits of reason, and applying these limits to considerations of religion. In the second case, "critique" means a reduction of religious transcendence to its purely anthropological meaning. But if it can be argued that Kantian "critique" yields a philosophy of religion that in the end is reducible to a moral anthropology of

religion, then Kant would have prepared the way for an anthropological critique of religion.

37. LPR, 28:1010–1011.

38. Reinhold, *Letters on the Kantian Philosophy*, 29, 44.

39. Jaeschke, *Reason in Religion*, 82.

40. CPJ, 5:475.

41. CPrR, 5:147.

42. CF, 7:38.

43. Ibid., 7:41–42.

44. Ibid., 7:42–43.

45. Ibid., 7:43–44.

46. Ibid., 7:40–41.

47. Ibid., 7:45.

48. Jaeschke, *Reason in Religion*, 79.

49. RL, 6:110–11.

Chapter 2

1. FK, 34.

2. Ibid., 35.

3. Ibid., 5.

4. Ibid., 4.

5. Ibid., 7–8.

6. Ibid., 8.

7. Ibid.

8. Ibid., 9.

9. Ibid., 10–11.

10. Ibid., 11.

11. It should be noted that, even though Derrida rightly sees this "death of God" as implied in the notion of a postulate of practical reason, this is not in fact the ethical interpretation of the Passion that Kant himself provides. In Part II of the *Religion*, Kant writes: "We cannot think the ideal of a humanity well pleasing to God (hence of such moral perfection as is possible to a being pertaining to this world and dependent on needs and inclinations) except in the idea of a human being willing not only to execute in person all human duties, and at the same time to spread goodness about him as far wide [sic] as possible through teaching and example, but also, though tempted by the greatest temptation, to take upon himself all sufferings, up to the most ignominious death, for the good of the world and even for his enemies.—For human beings cannot form for themselves any concept of the degree and the strength of a force like that of a moral disposition except by representing it surrounded by obstacles and yet—in the midst of the greatest possible temptations—victorious." RL, 6:61.

12. Nancy links the experience of the categorical imperative to an experience of radical abandonment to the law. See Nancy, *L'Imperatif categorique*, 141–53, translated in Nancy, *The Birth to Presence*, 36–47.

13. FK, 11–12.

14. Ibid., 12.

15. Ibid., 10; quotation marks are in the original.

16. RL, 6:52.

17. Ibid., 6:52–53.

18. TP, 56.

19. RL, 6:52.

20. FK, 10.

21. Ibid., 13.

22. Unfortunately, copyright issues prevent quotation from this unpublished material. What follows, therefore, is a paraphrase of Derrida's line of argument. Derrida's discussion of Kant takes place in the fourth section of the "*Religion et philosophie*" seminar, which is found in box 11, folders 14–19, of the Jacques Derrida Papers, Special Collections and Archives, The UC Irvine Libraries, Irvine, California.

23. RL, 6:168.

24. Ibid., 6:170–71.

25. On the development of the word "fetishism," see Iacono, *Le Fétichisme.* The word "fetish," which comes from the Latin *facticius* by way of the Portuguese *feitiço,* designates something artificial, fabricated by man from nature, and was applied by Europeans to the religious objects and cultic practices of the people of Guinea and western Africa in the fifteenth and sixteenth centuries. "Fetishism," however, as a concept belonging to a theory of "savage" or "primitive" religion, first appears in 1760 in Charles de Brosses, *Du culte des dieux fétiches.* See Iacono, *Le Fétichisme,* 5. This term was thus not very old when Kant used it in the *Religion.* Kant's usage is distinctive insofar as, anticipating in a way the employment of the concept by Marx and Freud, Kant relates it not to savage or primitive religion, but to "contemporary" cultural phenomena. Nevertheless, unlike Marx and Freud, Kant still uses this term specifically in the context of religion.

26. RL, 6:176–77.

27. Ibid., 6:178–79.

28. GL, 211.

29. Freud, "Fetishism," 198–99.

30. Ibid., 200.

31. Ibid., 201.

32. Ibid., 203.

33. Bennington, "Fetishism in *Glas,*" 195–96.

34. GL, 210. Sarah Kofman points out that Derrida's reading of Freud's text fails to acknowledge the fact that the fetish is not simply a substitute for the "thing itself," since the penis for which the fetish is a substitute is a "phantasmatic penis" which never appears as such. Hence in Freud's text the thing itself already involves an originary supplementarity. See Kofman, *Lectures de Derrida,* 132–39.

35. Freud, *Totem and Taboo,* xxvii.

36. Ibid., 29.

37. Another text relevant to the question of psychoanalysis and Kantian ethics is Freud's *New Introductory Lectures on Psycho-Analysis,* where he twice com-

ments on Kant's famous remark from the Conclusion to the second *Critique:* "Two things fill the mind with ever new and increasing admiration and reverence, the more often and more steadily one reflects on them: *the starry heavens above me and the moral law within me.*" CPrR, 5:161. See Freud, *New Introductory Lectures,* 77ff. and 202ff. Derrida also refers to Freud's comments in GL, 214.

38. GL, 206–7.

39. Ibid., 207.

40. Ibid., 211–12.

41. As Bennington notes, "We see, then, that Derrida is neither more nor less Hegelian than Kantian. *Glas* and the reading of Hegel no more give us the truth about Derrida than do the other texts, even if it is undeniable that the Hegelian weight bearing on all our thought can give *Glas* a contingent privilege in the formation of Derridean texts." Bennington, "Derridabase," 302.

42. Bennington, "Derridabase," especially 284–302, is perhaps the clearest reading of the main thrust and implications of *Glas* and Hegel more generally.

43. GL, 213.

44. Ibid., 215–16; the quotation marks are in the original.

45. Ibid., 217.

46. Ibid., 216.

Chapter 3

1. Bernasconi's work has influenced a number of attempts to determine the ethics of deconstruction, including Simon Critchley's *The Ethics of Deconstruction: Derrida and Levinas,* and Drucilla Cornell's *The Philosophy of the Limit.* I take the limitations of this approach to have been amply demonstrated by Martin Hägglund and will not belabor them here; my position on the question of "deconstruction and ethics" will nevertheless become clear in the course of this chapter. For an extensive critique of Bernasconi, Critchley, and Cornell, see Hägglund, "The Necessity of Discrimination: Disjoining Derrida and Levinas," 55ff., and the chapter based on this essay in his book *Radical Atheism.* As I will explain below, I nevertheless fundamentally disagree with certain key features of Hägglund's reading of Derrida.

2. VM, 96, 314.

3. Ibid., 123–24.

4. Ibid., 125.

5. GD, 68.

6. Hägglund, "Necessity of Discrimination," 56.

7. AD, 32.

8. Hägglund, "Necessity of Discrimination," 53.

9. AD, 33.

10. Laclau, *Emancipation(s),* 81, 77.

11. See, for example, Derrida's "Letter to a Japanese Friend": "[I]t must also be made clear that deconstruction is not even an *act* or an *operation.* [. . .] Not only because it does not return to an individual or collective *subject* who

would take the initiative and apply it to an object, a text, a theme, etc. Deconstruction is an event that does not await the deliberation, consciousness, or organization of a subject." LJ, 3–4.

12. FK, 8.

13. Laclau, *Emancipation(s),* 77–78.

14. Ibid., 70.

15. On the universal as "empty signifier," see Laclau, *Emancipation(s),* 36–46.

16. On this point, see Alain Badiou's denunciation of Levinasian ethics in *Ethics,* 18–29.

17. Rorty, "Remarks on Deconstruction," 16.

18. Ibid., 17.

19. Jenkins, "Gestures Beyond Tolerance," 128.

20. PM, 67.

21. PT, 129.

22. Hägglund, "Necessity of Discrimination," 67.

23. Hägglund, *Radical Atheism,* 231–32.

24. For an extensive critique of Hägglund's work along these lines, see Caputo, "The Return of Anti-Religion." Caputo does note, in fairness to Hägglund, Hägglund's disclaimer in the introduction to *Radical Atheism* to be taking an "analytic rather than exegetical" approach designed to "develop his arguments, fortify his logic, and pursue its implications." Hägglund, *Radical Atheism,* 11. While Hägglund is certainly within his rights to take this approach, it presupposes that one can know which passages in Derrida constitute the "inconsistencies." Moreover, while Hägglund gives himself license to not adhere slavishly to the letter of Derrida's text, he criticizes those who read Derrida on the basis of those passages he calls "inconsistent" with the logic of deconstruction with having *misread* Derrida. All of this relies upon an excessively healthy confidence in his own ability to sift out the true Derrida, faithful to the logic of deconstruction, from the "inconsistent" one.

25. LI, 152.

26. Ibid., 152–53.

27. PS, 9.

28. Ibid., 7.

29. Ibid., 9.

30. GW, 4:389.

31. Ibid., 4:393.

32. Ibid., 4:394.

33. Nietzsche, *Gay Science,* 205.

34. GW, 4:398.

35. Ibid., 4:398.

36. Ibid., 4:399–400.

37. Paton, *Categorical Imperative,* 46.

38. See, for example, the *Critique of Practical Reason,* where Kant writes: "The moral law is, in other words, for the will of a perfect being a law of *holiness,* but for the will of every finite rational being a law of *duty,* of moral necessitation

and of the determination of his actions through *respect* for this law and *reverence* for his duty." CPrR, 5:82.

39. CPrR, 5:71.

40. GW, 4:407.

41. PS, 142, n.12.

42. Ibid.

43. GW, 4:408–9.

44. Ibid., 4:409. Kant makes substantially the same point in Part II of the *Metaphysics of Morals* in his discussion of the teaching of ethics. Yet while Kant denies here that imitation can serve as the basis of morality, and asserts that examples serve to put beyond doubt the practicability of the law, Kant does hold a place for the example in the education of young children: "The *experimental* (technical) means for cultivating virtue is *good* example on the part of the teacher (his exemplary conduct) and *cautionary* example in others, since, for a still undeveloped human being, imitation is the first determination of his will to accept maxims that he afterwards makes for himself." MM, 6:479. See below on Kant's proximity to Rousseau on this point.

45. GW, 4:419.

46. PS, 141, n.10.

47. GR, 344–45, n.35.

48. Ibid., 205.

49. Ibid.

50. For a full examination of the problem of the example in Rousseau's pedagogy and Derrida's reading of Rousseau in *Of Grammatology*, see Harvey, *Labyrinths of Exemplarity*.

51. GW, 4:421.

52. Ibid., 4:429.

53. FL, 243, 249.

54. Ibid., 233.

55. Ibid., 250.

56. Ibid.

57. FL, 233.

58. MM, 6:229, 230, 232.

59. FL, 235.

60. Ibid., 258. For Derrida's comments on freedom, see *For What Tomorrow . . .* , his dialogue with Elisabeth Roudinesco, especially Chapter 4. Derrida discusses here his precautions concerning the word freedom, but then remarks that Jean-Luc Nancy's *The Experience of Freedom* represents "the only attempt, the most convincing effort to open a passage by which the word or concept of 'freedom' might be given a postdeconstructive virtue." WT, 51. Derrida offers a reading of *The Experience of Freedom* in *Rogues,* Part I. His reflections on questions of freedom and equality take place by way of an extensive re-evaluation of the concept of "democracy." On the question of democracy, see in particular *The Politics of Friendship.*

61. Concerning the signatures that sign the American Declaration of Independence in the name of the laws of nature and of God, Derrida writes: "They

pose or *posit* their institutional laws on the foundation of natural laws and by the same coup (the interpretive coup of force) in the name of God, creator of nature. He comes, in effect, to guarantee the rectitude of popular intentions, the unity and goodness of the people. He founds natural laws and the whole game which tends to present performative utterances *as* constative utterances." DI, 8. It is precisely the performativity of the founding of the law that Derrida will emphasize in "Force of Law."

62. FL, 241–42.

63. In "Declarations of Independence," Derrida provides an analysis of the American Declaration of Independence in terms of the performative utterance and the performativity of the signature. Concerning the declarative act that founds an institution, Derrida writes: "Such an act does not come back to a constative or descriptive discourse. It performs, it accomplishes, it does what it says it does: that at least would be its intentional structure. Such an act does not have the same relation to its presumed signer—to whatever subject, individual or collective, engages itself in producing it—as a text of the 'constative' type, if in all rigor there are any 'constative' texts and if one could come across them in 'science,' in 'philosophy,' or in 'literature.' The declaration which founds an institution, a constitution or a State requires that a signer engage him- or herself. The signature maintains a link with the instituting act, as an act of language and of writing, a link which has absolutely nothing of the empirical accident about it." DI, 8. For Derrida's reading of Austin's distinction between performative and constative utterances and the relationship between performativity and the signature, see "Signature Event Context" in *Limited Inc.*

64. Quoted in FL, 240.

65. FL, 242.

66. Ibid., 243.

67. Ibid., 254.

68. Ibid., 248.

69. Ibid., 250–51.

70. Quoted in FL, 238.

71. FL, 239, 241.

72. Ibid., 244.

73. Ibid., 251.

74. Ibid., 253.

75. Ibid.

76. PS, 15.

77. Ibid.

78. Ibid., 16–17.

Chapter 4

1. FK, 1.

2. Ibid., 23.

3. Ibid., 26.

4. GD, 68.
5. FK, 33, 37, 36.
6. Ibid., 26.
7. Austin, *How to Do Things,* 5.
8. Ibid., 21–22.
9. Ibid., 15.
10. SE, 325–26.
11. Austin, *How to Do Things,* 151.
12. FK, 63–64.
13. Austin, *How to Do Things,* 148.
14. See Grice, *Studies in the Way of Words.*
15. In this text, Derrida examines Husserl's distinction between expressive and indicative signs, and, specifically, Husserl's inability to eliminate all deixis from "presence to oneself."
16. FK, 44.
17. UG, 276.
18. FK, 41, 47.
19. Fenves, "Out of the Blue," 126.
20. FK, 65.
21. Quoted by Kant in SRL, 8:425.
22. SRL, 8:425.
23. Fenves, "Politics of Friendship," 133.
24. SRL, 8:426.
25. OH, 67, 69, 71–73.
26. SRL, 8:427.
27. FK, 33.
28. Ibid., 37.
29. Ibid., 49.
30. Ibid., 50, 49.
31. Ibid., 58.
32. Ibid., 49, 48, 50.
33. Ibid., 50–51.
34. Ibid., 52.
35. For a preliminary attempt to answer this question, see Miller, "Derrida and the Problem of the Secularized Messianic," upon which much of this section is based.
36. Quoted from Caputo, *Prayers and Tears,* 117.
37. FL, 254.
38. RR, 83–84.
39. Ibid., 84, 85.
40. On the connection of "form" to the metaphysics of presence, see SP, 62–63, as well as FM.
41. FK, 17–18.
42. OU, 34.
43. GR, 5. Derrida uses the image of monstrosity in the closing lines of "Structure, Sign, and Play" as well, where he speaks of the "as yet unnamable

which is proclaiming itself and which can do so, as is necessary whenever a birth is in the offing, only under the species of the nonspecies, in the formless, mute, infant, and terrifying form of monstrosity." SS, 293.

44. FK, 18.
45. MS, 254–55.
46. FK, 16.
47. Ibid., 14.
48. MS, 255.
49. FK, 21.
50. Hart, "Encyclopedias and Other Things," 60.
51. FL, 254.
52. Caputo, *Prayers and Tears,* 142.
53. FK, 21–22.
54. Ibid., 22.
55. Voltaire, *Philosophical Dictionary,* 390.
56. Ibid., 390–91.
57. Ibid., 393.
58. Ibid.
59. Ibid., 392–94.
60. For a reading of Locke's *Letter Concerning Toleration* in terms of this opposition between "inner" and "outer," see Fish, "Mission Impossible."
61. RL, 6:123.
62. FK, 29–30.
63. Ibid., 8.
64. Ibid., 22.
65. RR, 142.

Bibliography

Works by Derrida and Kant are cited in full in the abbreviations, pp. 105–108.

Austin, J. L. *How to Do Things with Words.* Edited by J. O. Urmson and Marina Sbisà. Cambridge: Harvard University Press, 1975.

Badiou, Alain. *Ethics: An Essay on the Understanding of Radical Evil.* Translated by Peter Hallward. New York: Verso, 2001.

Beiser, Frederick. *The Fate of Reason: German Philosophy from Kant to Fichte.* Cambridge: Harvard University Press, 1987.

Bennington, Geoffrey. "Derridabase." In *Jacques Derrida.* Chicago: University of Chicago Press, 1993.

———. "Fetishism in *Glas.*" In *Other Analyses: Reading Philosophy.* 2004: PDF e-book (available from www.bennington.zsoft.co.uk).

———. *Legislations: The Politics of Deconstruction.* New York: Verso, 1994.

Bernasconi. Robert. "The Trace of Levinas in Derrida." In *Derrida and* Différance. Edited by David Wood and Robert Bernasconi, 13–29. Evanston: Northwestern University Press, 1988.

Caputo, John D. *The Prayers and Tears of Jacques Derrida: Religion without Religion.* Bloomington: Indiana University Press, 1997.

———. "The Return of Anti-Religion: From Radical Atheism to Radical Theology." *Journal for Cultural and Religious Theory* 11, no. 2 (2011): 32–125. http://www.jcrt.org/archives/11.2/caputo.pdf.

Collins, James. *The Emergence of Philosophy of Religion.* New Haven: Yale University Press, 1967.

Cornell, Drucilla. *The Philosophy of the Limit.* New York: Routledge, 1992.

Critchley, Simon. *The Ethics of Deconstruction: Derrida and Levinas.* 2nd ed. West Lafayette: Purdue University Press, 1999.

Despland, Michael. *Kant on History and Religion.* Montreal: McGill-Queen's University Press, 1973.

Di Giovanni, George. Introduction to *The Main Philosophical Writings and the Novel* Allwill, by Friedrich Heinrich Jacobi. Translated by George di Giovanni. Montreal & Kingston: McGill-Queen's University Press, 1994.

Dupré, Louis. *A Dubious Heritage: Studies in the Philosophy of Religion after Kant.* New York: Paulist Press, 1977.

Fenves, Peter. Review of *L'Impératif catégorique,* by Jean-Luc Nancy. *Modern Language Notes* 100 (1985): 1136–39.

———. *Late Kant: Towards Another Law of the Earth.* New York: Routledge, 2003.

———. "Out of the Blue: Secrecy, Radical Evil, and the Crypt of Faith." In *Futures: Of Jacques Derrida.* Edited by Richard Rand. Stanford: Stanford University Press, 2001.

———. "Politics of Friendship—Once Again." *Eighteenth-Century Studies* 32 (1998): 133–55.

Fish, Stanley. "Mission Impossible: Settling the Just Bounds between Church and State." *Columbia Law Review* 97 (1997): 2255–2333.

Förster, Eckart. *Kant's Final Synthesis: An Essay on the* Opus postumum. Cambridge: Harvard University Press, 2000.

Freud, Sigmund. "Fetishism." In *Collected Papers.* Edited by James Strachey. Translated by Joan Riviere, vol. 5. London: Hogarth Press, 1953.

———. *New Introductory Lectures on Psycho-Analysis.* Translated by James Strachey. New York: Norton, 1965.

———. *Totem and Taboo.* Translated by James Strachey. New York: Norton, 1950.

Greisch, Jean. *Le Buisson ardent et les Lumières de la raison: Héritages et héritiers du XIXe siècle.* Vol. 1. Paris: Éditions du Cerf, 2002.

Grice, Paul. *Studies in the Way of Words.* Cambridge: Harvard University Press, 1989.

Guyer, Paul. "From a Practical Point of View: Kant's Conception of a Postulate of Pure Practical Reason." Chapter 10 in *Kant on Freedom, Law, and Happiness.* New York: Cambridge University Press, 2000.

Hägglund, Martin. "The Necessity of Discrimination: Disjoining Derrida and Levinas." *Diacritics* 34 (2004): 40–71.

———. *Radical Atheism: Derrida and the Time of Life.* Stanford: Stanford University Press, 2008.

Hart, Kevin. "Encyclopedias and Other Things: Some Recent Theology." *Journal for Cultural and Religious Theory* 6 (2005): 43–69.

Harvey, Irene E. *Derrida and the Economy of* Différance. Bloomington: Indiana University Press, 1986.

———. *Labyrinths of Exemplarity: At the Limits of Deconstruction.* Albany: State University of New York Press, 2002.

Husserl, Edmund. *Ideas Pertaining to a Pure Phenomenology and to a Phenomenological Philosophy: First Book.* Translated by F. Kersten. Norwell, MA: Kluwer, 1998.

Iacono, Alfonso M. *Le Fétichisme: histoire d'un concept.* Paris: Press Universitaires de France, 1992.

Jaeschke, Walter. *Reason in Religion: The Foundations of Hegel's Philosophy of Religion.* Translated by J. Michael Stewart and Peter C. Hodgson. Berkeley: University of California Press, 1990.

Jenkins, Fiona. "Gestures Beyond Tolerance: Generosity, Fatality, and the Logic of the State." *Angelaki: A Journal of the Theoretical Humanities* 7 (2002): 119–29.

Kates, Joshua. *Essential History: Jacques Derrida and the Development of Deconstruction.* Evanston: Northwestern University Press, 2005.

Kofman, Sarah. *Lectures de Derrida.* Paris: Éditions Galilée, 1984.

Laclau, Ernesto. *Emancipation(s).* New York: Verso, 2007.

Lawlor, Leonard. *Derrida and Husserl: The Basic Problem of Phenomenology.* Bloomington: Indiana University Press, 2002.

Lessing, Gotthold Ephraim. "The Education of the Human Race." In *Philosophical and Theological Writings*. Edited by H. B. Nisbet. New York: Cambridge University Press, 2005.

Levinas, Emmanuel. "Jacques Derrida: Wholly Otherwise." In *Proper Names*. Translated by Michael B. Smith, 55–62. Stanford: Stanford University Press, 1996.

———. *Otherwise Than Being, or Beyond Essence*. Translated by Alphonso Lingis. Pittsburgh: Duquesne University Press, 1998.

Mariña, Jacqueline. "Kant on Grace: A Reply to His Critics." *Religious Studies* 33 (1997): 379–400.

Marrati, Paola. *Genesis and Trace: Derrida Reading Husserl and Heidegger*. Stanford: Stanford University Press, 2005.

Michalson, Gordon. *Fallen Freedom: Kant on Radical Evil and Moral Regeneration*. New York: Cambridge University Press, 1990.

Miller, Eddis. "Derrida and the Problem of the Secularized Messianic." In *On the Outlook: Figures of the Messianic*. Edited by Thomas Crombez and Katrien Vloeberghs, 35–43. Newcastle, UK: Cambridge Scholars Publishing, 2007.

Naas, Michael. *Miracle and Machine: Jacques Derrida and the Two Sources of Religion, Science, and the Media*. New York: Fordham University Press, 2012.

Nancy, Jean-Luc. *The Birth to Presence*. Translated by Brian Holmes et al. Stanford: Stanford University Press, 1993.

———. *L'impératif catégorique*. Paris: Flammarion, 1983.

Nietzsche, Friedrich. *The Gay Science*. Translated by Walter Kaufmann. New York: Vintage, 1974.

Paton, H. J. *The Categorical Imperative: A Study in Kant's Moral Philosophy*. Philadelphia: University of Pennsylvania Press, 1971.

Reinhold, Karl Leonhard. *Letters on the Kantian Philosophy*. Edited by Karl Ameriks. Translated by James Hebbeler. New York: Cambridge University Press, 2005.

Ricoeur, Paul. "A Philosophical Hermeneutics of Religion: Kant." In *Figuring the Sacred: Religion, Narrative, Imagination*. Edited by Mark I. Wallace. Translated by David Pellauer, 77–92. Minneapolis: Fortress Press, 1995.

Rorty, Richard. "Remarks on Deconstruction and Pragmatism." In *Deconstruction and Pragmatism*. Edited by Chantal Mouffe, 13–17. New York: Routledge, 1996.

Shakespeare, Steven. *Derrida and Theology*. New York: Continuum, 2009.

Voltaire. *Philosophical Dictionary*. Edited and translated by Theodore Besterman. London: Penguin, 1972.

Wood, Allen W. *Kant's Moral Religion*. Ithaca: Cornell University Press, 1970.

———. *Kant's Rational Theology*. Ithaca: Cornell University Press, 1978.

Index